CU00923896

DARK PSYCHOLOGY

Learn How To Analyze People and Defend Yourself from Emotional Influence, Brainwashing and Deception

by Dylan Black

© Copyright 2020
All rights reserved

This book is targeted towards offering important details about the subject covered. The publication is being provided with the thought that the publisher is not mandated to render an accounting or other qualified services. If recommendations are needed, professional or legal, a practiced person in the profession ought to be engaged.

In no way is it legal to recreate, duplicate, or transfer any part of this document in either electronic means or printed format. Copying of this publication is strictly prohibited or storage of this document is not allowed. Unless, with written authorization from the publisher. All rights reserved.

The details supplied here are specified to be honest and constant. Because any liability, in regards to inattention or otherwise, by any usage or abuse of any directions, processes, or policies confined within is the sole and utter obligation of the recipient reader. Under no circumstances will any form of legal duty or blame be held against the publisher for any reparation, damages, or financial loss due to the information herein, either directly or indirectly. The author owns all copyrights not held by the publisher.

The information herein is provided for educational purpose exclusively and is universal. The presentation of the data is without contractual agreement or any kind of warranty assurance.

All trademarks inside this book are for clarifying purposes only and are possessed by the owners themselves, not allied with this document.

Disclaimer

All erudition supplied in this book is specified for educational and academic purpose only. The author is not in any way in charge for any outcomes that emerge from utilizing this book. Constructive efforts have been made to render information that is both precise and effective, however the author is not to be held answerable for the accuracy or use/misuse of this information.

Foreword

I will like to thank you for taking the very first step of trusting me and deciding to purchase/read this life-transforming book. Thanks for investing your time and resources on this product.

I can assure you of precise outcomes if you will diligently follow the specific blueprint I lay bare in the information handbook you are currently checking out. It has transformed lives, and I strongly believe it will equally transform your own life too.

All the information I provided in this Do It Yourself piece is easy to absorb and practice.

Table of Contents

INTRODUCTION

Do you feel like you are a pawn in another person's chess video game? Are you tired of being manipulated at every point in time? Would you like to be able to spot and discern real feelings in others so that you can protect yourself from being emotionally abused and controlled? This is just the book you need. Dark Psychology: The Practical Uses and Best Defences of Psychological Warfare in Everyday Life assists you in knowing more than merely the basics of human behavior. It takes you on an in-depth journey that checks out the darker recesses of the human mind and provides informative, useful actions on how to develop your mental defences against such.

Inside this book, you will find out:

- Fundamental truths about dark psychology

- When it has been masked masterfully in a web of lies, how to acknowledge and separate reality

- Elements of your day to day life that makes you vulnerable to the controls of others

- If you've ever found yourself a victim, a five-step program to help you break free

- How to secure yourself from the impacts of dark psychology

If you or any of your loved ones have suffered emotionally or are presently living through a problem that is directly related to the intrinsic risks of dark psychology, this is a book you need to check out. And if you are just curious about how dark psychology works and would like to know how to safeguard yourself, this is a book that breaks down this complex phenomenon in the simplest terms.

Dark psychology is not a unique concept, so, this book is not about any groundbreaking discoveries. However, it has been discussed in hushed tones, and there is still a lot of information out there that has gotten lost in hardly reasonable psychobabble that leaves you more perplexed than notified.

This book does a reliable task of debunking dark psychology and equips you with the knowledge that you can use to safeguard yourself against it.

If you're all set, turn over to the next page and get ready to change your life.

CHAPTER ONE

What is dark psychology?

"It can not be seen, can not be felt, can not be heard, can not be smelt It hides behind stars and under hills and empty holes it fills It comes initially and follows after. Ends life, kills laughter."

J.R.R Tolkien - *The Hobbit*

The mind is among the most complicated aspects of human nature. The operations of the brain are something that has puzzled and fascinated mankind that we can remember. Scientists, theorists, and psychologists have sought to unwind the mysteries of the mind. It is a typically held belief that the human mind influences our habits and actions. A lot of research study work has gone to understanding the psychological process that a person goes through before taking action, whether good or bad.

Some are trying to study the human mind have focused efforts on the brain. These studies look at the physical elements of the brain with a concentrate on how details are gotten, processed, analyzed, and saved. Mainly, they want to get a much better understanding of how the mind can affect an individual's way of reasoning. It is studies like these have paved the way for development in managing debilitating conditions like Alzheimer's, perception troubles, and memory loss.

The more familiar aspect of the research study of the human mind is psychology. At some time in our lives, it is either we have spoken with a psychologist, or we knew someone who needed to consult one to peruse our harder psychological battles. Most times, life's experiences break us down in methods we can not fix on our own. Sometimes, the breakdown is as an outcome of specific biological markers we inherited from our parents. Feelings like depression, stress, and anxiety and fear, darken our everyday experiences makes it challenging to thrive. With a mix of drugs and treatment, we can secure ourselves from the darkness within.

What about the darkness in others?

Everyone has the capability of doing fantastic good. We likewise possess the ability to do exotic evil. Beneath feelings like sadness, depression, joy, there is a deep flared desire that can lead us to harm others if those advises intentionally are not brought under control. These darker desires are rooted in more primitive impulses like our flight or battle response that promotes our survival. In some cases, there is just one word that certifies the human response to these dark emotions evil.

Dark psychology is a research study of the human condition with the rational nature of human beings to prey on others.

In layman terms, dark psychology checks out that aspect of humanity that allows us intentionally to do something that brings damage to our fellow human beings. Mind you, the usage of the word victim in this context does not necessarily mean the physical harming of an individual. However, there is a branch of dark psychology that is dedicated to this. In subsequent chapters, we will touch briefly on those areas to get a much better understanding of the subject.

In films or books, you may have come across words or phrases pointing to "darkness within." Even a few of the most well-known philosophers made referrals to this. The revered book of the Christians discusses how "the heart of man is frantically wicked." We have all come across somebody who we have explained as remarkably calm or booked in social settings just for this same individual to commit an act so sneaky that we find it difficult to link that action with this person in question. Often, we are that person. As unexpected as it might look, it is not completely shocking.

Those cases are simply set off actions to external circumstances. The pot was stirred, so to speak and those dark feelings that hid underneath simmered to the surface. Typically they decline once control is applied. Everybody has a latent tendency to be a bit naughty or downright evil if the right "buttons" are pressed.

Some people on the other hand are in control of these dark feelings. They support them, feed them, and when it serves their purposes, they intentionally unleash them at the expense of another person.

Often, these emotions are groomed from an early age. A child discovers that if he or she weeps in a specific way, the adults around them rush to do their request. If the moms and dads do not like the child early enough the wrongness of this, the child matures believing individuals in their lives can be manipulated into meeting their request. The sobbing would cease to be a weapon as they grow, but they would continue in their manipulative ways. Where they don't use tears, they use emotions to blackmail their victims. So, what started as an innocent childish habit becomes a dark requirement to manage.

The lengths that this person would go to exert their control would define the strength of their actions. Dark psychology is everything about studying the thought procedure of an individual like this. It seeks to understand the intention behind these actions, and the patterns showed before these acts are brought out to after and tosses more light on how an individual can intentionally see those actions to conclusion understanding the hurt and pain it may trigger to another person.

Dark psychology brightens the dark side of humanity.

CHAPTER TWO

The Effects And Impact Of Dark Psychology

"When you light candlelight, you also cast a shadow" - Ursula K. Le Guin

Given the little we now know about dark psychology, we understand that a few of the most stunning criminal offenses are rooted in particular characteristics associated with dark psychology. But that is a broader negative effect. I wish to bring it closer to the house, to you and me.

How does this dark psychology affect us if it affects us at all?

I can guarantee you that there are no "ifs" to this question, and in a short time we would understand how.

The results of dark psychology are experienced by both the victim and the wrongdoer. To know the impacts, we need to explore some components of dark psychology. People who show a particular characteristic that is thought about dark such as narcissism, psychopathy, and Machiavellianism, are susceptible to experiencing difficulties in all aspects of their relationships. They have a higher propensity to dedicate a crime if all three qualities are present in one person. The three characteristics discussed have particular attributes that are grouped under them.

Narcissism, for instance, is identified by a sense of privilege, feelings of supremacy, deep seethed envy of the success of others, and exploitative behavior.

Psychopathy means a lack of regret, lack of compassion, devastating spontaneous habits, egocentricity, and failure to accept responsibility as a few of the attributes. Selfishness, ruthlessness, and manipulative practices are signs of Machiavellian characteristics. Individually, these characteristics are problematic but assembled; they can spell trouble, particularly in a person's relationship with others.

In the workplace, for instance, that person would:

- Underperform in the workplace even with the most ordinary jobs

- Interrupt workflow due to their failure to agree with others
- Would be incredibly done not like by others
- Their impulsivity would lead them to make doubtful choices that are not ethical
- If put in an administrative capacity, they are more likely to dedicate a clerical crime

But it is not merely their work relationships that suffer.

In their relationships, they are bound to encounter the following issues:

- Their constant need for attention and recognition can be tiring for their partner leading to the faster breakup of the relationships
- They turn to emotional and physical blackmails to manipulate their partners
- They tend to be either verbally, emotionally or physically abusive with their kids or partners
- Individuals who enter into relationships with them pay a high emotional cost

If you have encountered a person whose relationships are identified by these experiences, for the sake of your peace of mind and general wellness, avoid them. If, on the other hand, you are the one who experiences this, seek the mental assistance you need to get better. No matter how deep-rooted these problems are, you can enhance your behavior and experiences with the best form of therapy. The initial step is acknowledging the circumstance for what it is, admit that you have a problem, and look for help without delay.

For the rest of us, dealing with people who have the traits I discussed above leaves us mentally and psychologically distress. In some cases, the impact can be physical and, in extreme cases, fatal. The sweet neighbor whose horrible experience led me on this journey to writing this book lost everything physically; her home, her company, her finances, but her loss was much more profound and higher than these. We didn't have a relationship with the criminal of the act; but, we ended up being victims.

Our losses were not as huge as hers; but, we experienced loss too. For beginners, we lost our sweet next-door neighbor. She didn't die but she never recuperated from the experience.

We lost our capability to trust strangers. Even our relationships with each other seemed to require an extra layer of trust to flourish.

The greatest effect of dark psychology on anyone is that it produces a strong sense of loss. We lose our valuables, we lose relationships, we lose ourselves [I will describe that in a bit] and for those who are very regrettable, they lose their lives. It is safe to say that the impact of this darkness is profound.

According to specialists, if a person shows one of the dark personality types, there is a very high propensity that the person would show the others. In essential society, if the more significant members of the community exhibit these traits, it is safe to say that the criminal offense perpetration rates because society would be considerably high. That is not to say that people living in cities or countries with more criminal offenses are more criminally inclined. There are other contributing factors to be considered. The possibility can not be completely ruled out either.

Something that can not be eliminated though is the causal sequence of actions directly associated with or as a result of dark character traits. There particular damaging behaviors that turn victims into predators, too, and this cycle continues well to the future until someone plucks up the guts and takes the vibrant step to break complimentary. Children from violent houses, for instance, usually grow up to be abusers. Sometimes, in their effort to break away from their adult mold, they find themselves trapped in similarly abusive relationships even if they are not the abusers themselves. If they have a powerful gravitational pull towards the violent elements that characterized their childhood house, it is practical.

For some others, ending up being victims can have such a significant effect on their psyche that it causes something in them to snap. I have read that; "snapping" can be temporary. In a brief minute, they lose control over all their primitive instincts and act on the most energetic feeling that surfaces, which is typically anger. This condition is what causes some people to plead momentary madness. But some people accept the dark emotions that surface when they "snap." All sense of morality goes out of the window. The aftermath of this is usually devastating.

CHAPTER THREE

Day To Day Examples Of Different Aspects Of Dark Psychology

"I am scared of this dark thing that sleeps in me; All day, I feel its soft feathery turnings, its malignity " - Sylvia Plath, ***Ariel***

When you think about dark habits, you would be forgiven for thinking that it only applies to any criminal activity that lands you on the front page of the dailies or becomes a feature-length movie on the illegal activity channel. In reality, it likewise includes instead a variety of things that have typically become socially appropriate even if we do not condone such habits personally. We witness these actions in our homes, schools, and workplaces to innovative technology, we now see it on the internet. To help you get a brighter image and a much deeper understanding of this subject as well as telling you how close these actions are, I am going to show you a few of the most sensational criminal offenses stories and the seemingly insignificant activities the led to an awful end.

CASE STUDY ONE

News: Brutal Murder of a 14-year-old boy

Traits of the Perpetrator: Controlling, Violent, Manipulative, Reclusive

Channel: Online Gaming

This was the terrible story of a young boy from a well-grounded home; he had the same benefits of any teen in the same age and social group, he had a supportive mommy and a daddy who strived to give. His mom took all the required precautions a mom would safeguard her kid from the intrusive world of the web. Online video gaming was just another thing any young teenage boy would love. As long as he didn't invest more than the proper time on it, he ought to be okay.

The perpetrator, who was only four years older, had ominous plans. By thoroughly manipulating his impressionable and young victim with lies, he fooled the young boy into visiting him at his place where he engaged the vicious criminal activity. It was among the most disturbing cases, especially when you think about the age of the victim and the perpetrator. Regardless of his generation, the perpetrator displayed all the predatory characteristics linked to dark psychology and snuffed out life to assert control.

CASE STUDY TWO

News: Worst Domestic Violence Case

Traits of the Perpetrator: Physically, Violent, Manipulative, Controlling

Channel: Relationship

Love is indeed a beautiful thing. You go into it with the hopes that this person would like and care for you when you enter into a relationship with somebody that you would support and secure each other. In the modern-day love language, it is you and the person versus the world. And indeed, it started this way in this relationship. A single mother is striving to care for and offer her daughter to captivating boy who was what she had always wished in a man.

He was lovely, thoughtful, and appeared to like her boy just as much as he wanted her. To make himself readily available for this young family, he quit his job and dedicated himself to taking care of her until his real dark nature emerged. Using her love for her family, he manipulated her into isolating herself from those closest to her. He orchestrated the loss of her job, which led to the loss of her home. This made sure that she was based on him. He relocated her to his own house, where she was constantly subjected to round the clock abuse that included some of the most inhumane treatments.

His careful manipulation of the female as so reliable that when he gave her the choice of how she wishes to be eliminated, she mulled the thought over because she felt she had no option and was worthy of no betterment. Chance and an act of bravery on her part resulted in her rescue and imprisonment of the criminal.

CASE STUDY THREE

News: A popular Minister of God accused of molesting under aged members

Characteristics of the Perpetrator: Manipulative, controlling, egocentric

Channel: Religion

There is a spiritual relationship between religious leaders and their fans. The leader is indicated to be the moral compass that directs the followers appropriately to lead their lives. For years, despite religious beliefs, leaders have abused their position of power choosing instead to play out the biblical recommendation of to proverbial sheep and shepherd role. Other than being shepherds, they choose to be wolves.

Having established his credibility by declaring to have direct communication with God, this spiritual leader tricked his members with his vision. At some time, he proclaimed himself God and claimed he had to sleep with seven virgins, which also happened to be minors. He was later credited court and convicted of the crime.

These three cases here are mind-blowing, but the lesson is what I want to call your attention to. These crimes were not random, spur of the time kind of criminal activities. It involved careful orchestration that groomed the victims and pulled them because of the false state of trust and security before they struck. The way the occasions played out evokes the role-play between a predator and its victim. The victim is stalked and observed based on the details obtained during the observation process, and the predator makes a move. Just this move is not to strike but to charm their prey. Make them feel liked and cared for. It looks like they use a mask and portray characteristics that they know attract their victims.

Gradually, trust is established. The next objective is to get their prey to depend on them. Whether it is financial reliance, emotional dependence, or spiritual reliance, the outcome is the same. They wish to feel needed. They separate their victim, after which, they strike. It is not like those criminal activities that you suspect or see coming far away. It is like a song and dance regimen that offers the predator the advantage and leaves the victim vulnerable. In the next chapter, we will discuss how vulnerable we are.

CHAPTER FOUR

How Sensitive Are We To Dark Psychology?

"To share your weakness is to make yourself vulnerable; to make yourself vulnerable is to show your strength." - Criss Jami

The concern of our vulnerability comes to the leading edge if we analyze the case research studies used to show the effects of dark psychology in our daily life. The channels these perpetrators used are rather innocent and not precisely what one would classify as a precursor to doom. So, it is safe to say that it is the premises on which platforms were used that led to the poor outcome. In the very first case, you have a kid in a video gaming chat room for his peers. His passion for the video game brought him there; but, it was his need to connect with friends that informed his choices, and it was this requirement that the predator preyed.

In the 2nd case research study, it was a fundamental human right to get in touch with somebody on an intimate level that was preyed on, and the feelings of the victim were controlled to change her reality. From love, she came down into an emotional state of insignificance, and the wrongdoer inflicted more harm on her because of her vulnerable state.

And in the 3rd case, the victims placed their faith in the wrong deity even though their objectives were right and human. The predator presented himself as a crucial link to what they wanted to attain spiritually, and this desire ended up being the facility for their doom.

Other cases I have studied follows this same pattern. The wishes and emotional needs of the victims were weaved against them. This gives credence to the belief that our desires and needs are what make us vulnerable to these predators. Does this line of knowledge mean we should shut ourselves down emotionally? Let us give this more thought.

We have been raised to show strength, not to give in, and not to allow anybody see our worries. That is because we are taught that going against these directions would result in people seeing us as weak and vulnerable.

Paradoxically, it is the very thing that separates us from other animals that have also end up being the real source of both our strength and weakness. And that thing is our humanity. Because we are human, we are vulnerable. Our desires, our hopes, our aspirations, our quest for living a transcendent life are a few of the essential things that make us vulnerable.

The day we cease to possess any of these things, we stop to be human, and when we are no longer human, we end up being the thing that we are trying to protect ourselves against. When we stop thinking, when we stop caring, or when we stop being vulnerable, we become these soulless people whose sole objective is to satisfy their wanton desires with ruthlessness regardless of who would be harmed in the process. That said, while we acknowledge that our humanity makes us vulnerable, we must not forget that we can also draw strength from it.

This brings me to the biologically deep-rooted need for humans to get in touch with others. Acknowledge that this need is a healthy emotional human need. Without a connection with another human, we stop functioning well.

We need contact with other humans to grow. Since individuals have different reasons for establishing relationships with others, this need to connect with others makes us vulnerable.

Some are genuinely aiming to build good relationships, some simply want to use people in their lives to get some other objective or goals like wealth or influence. For some others, their intentions are even more sinister. The secret to navigating this type of human agenda is understand it.

There was a time that the saying "Ignorance is bliss" was touted in many circles as a mantra to put focus on the problem of the responsibility that comes with knowledge. I can assure you that the cost you incur for lack of knowledge is far higher than the burden that understanding brings. And if you wish to win this mental warfare against the enticing impacts of dark psychology, you need knowledge and the ideal application of knowledge in what you do.

Giving up on having feelings may appear like the perfect option, but there are documented cases where this resulted and backfired in even higher losses. Choosing to be dishonest and being reclusive made the victims much more prone and vulnerable to a vicious predatory attack.

Instead of shutting down opportunities to develop relationships with others, you ought to remain open but be cautious when it comes to your needs and feelings. I am likewise familiar with cases where the victim's emotional needs subdued their rational thinking. And this is what put them in damage's way. Our emotions can function as a navigational system that guides us to our needs and there are particular feelings that work as biological defences against risks like the ones we have been considering. And as we check out the subject in details, you will learn what those emotions are, in addition to how to train yourself to acknowledge them. Until then, if you are taking anything away from this chapter, it must be the understanding that yes, you are vulnerable. But, by acknowledging and welcoming those vulnerabilities, you can reverse your most significant weak points into your greatest strength.

CHAPTER FIVE

Analyzing Dark Psychology Manipulation

"Manipulation sustained with great intent can be a true blessing. However, when used wickedly, it is the beginning of a magician's karmic calamity." - T. F. Hodge

In plain terms, to control someone is to control or affect that person skilfully or unscrupulously. Like it or not, we have all manipulated somebody or a scenario for a desirable outcome. It sounds dark but, let me lighten the state of mind with a story from my mischievous youth.

As a child, I had a practice of conveniently falling sick when I didn't wish to go to school. Initially, my parents would fawn at me whenever this happened. After two emergency trips to the center, my mother thought of my mischiefs. The next few times after that, I wasn't taken to the center; however, I was allowed to stay home. Throughout one of my tummy episodes, my pals called me excitedly to inform me that a regional actor was coming to the school for a check-up. I went to my mom pleading to be taken back to school, forgetting that I had "unbearable stomach pain". My mum told me she wasn't going to make any opportunities and that I ought to sit tight. No quantity pleading could change her mind. Not even after I confessed to fabricating my stomach pains. When I got to school the next day, I was green with envy when my friends showed me all the cool things the mister actor brought for them. Suffice it to state, and I never fabricated sickness to get out of school.

When it comes to the things that we do to control a circumstance, this story is simply one out of many. I still understand many grownups who fake a cold to get a day off work. That is not entirely bad, is it? In some cases, we have been manipulated into making choices that are beneficial to us. A friend gives you a nice pair of running shoes and a one-month membership to a local health club, you know they want you to step up in the physical fitness department. Ever appeared at a lunch date with a friend only for an emergency and a potential partner (for your friend obviously) to reveal up? I have been there. Interestingly, when we feel threatened, one of the techniques we employ to get out of that undesirable situation if blunt force is not an option; this is also manipulation.

That is to say, the art of manipulation belongs to our nature. However, when it comes to psychological manipulation, things get darker and more evil. In this situation, an individual's actions or ideas are affected by making use of deceptive methods that are either violent, misleading or both. In this context, the person who is being manipulated isn't offered the option to either accept or decline the desire of the manipulator. They are simply coerced into compliance.

Manipulators have their reasons for doing what they do. Often, it is something as standard as getting financial gains like the imaginary soldier who duped my neighbor of all her life savings. In the work environment, these individuals are committed to advancing their agenda, even if it would result in hitting some heads against each other. Their concept is fundamental; if you desire it, you have to reach out and take it. In relationships, it is typically about getting power and staying in control. The need to be in charge of fuel whatever they do, and in some cases, they can go extreme lengths to achieve this. And after that, you have who love to control people for leisure purposes. They are just tired, and they use their manipulative video games to pass the time. It is crude and vicious; however, this is just the way they think.

One of the most common tactics used by manipulators is lying. A master manipulator is competent in the art of deceptiveness. They are adept at creating grand stories that have no real bearings on the fact. Or they choose subterfuge and lie by omission. Some people are so good at their lies that you practically never realize the lie until it is far too late. Another tactic employed by manipulators is regret tripping and shaming. When faced with something they have done wrong, they would immediately deny it and then quickly turn the tables around by making you feel bad for questioning them in the first place. To further reinforce their hang on their victim, they vilify them, thus effectively turning the victim into the abuser. You would see this type of manipulative technique in domestic cases where the abuser would claim that the victim's character, words, or actions are what triggered their behavior in the first place.

Other subtle strategies used in manipulation, consists of the use of evasive, non-committal reactions to concerns asked.

Rationalizing actions if they are captured and spinning the reality to match their narrative. Some manipulators use sex and seduction to bring out their sneaky goals. When caught with their hands in the proverbial cookie jar, anger and projection of blame are rapidly used to control the scenario in their favor.

Nevertheless, manipulators are not always random in their choice of victim. There are particular traits in their victims that attracts them, and specific vulnerabilities also make it easier for the manipulator to commit their crimes. Lonely people with lousy self-esteem and an eagerness to please are easier to manage than a certain social type. Some people exhibit characteristics that are comparable to the later on who ends up being manipulated. For such people, manipulators study their character defects and weaknesses before using it against them. Impressionable people are likely to be fooled by appearances. Bold people who tend to make compulsive decisions are likely to be controlled into making breeze choices that have long term effects. People who are materialistic and greedy have a higher tendency of being scammed.

CHAPTER SIX

Deception

"Just because something isn't a lie, it does not mean that it isn't misleading. A liar knows that he is a liar. But one who speaks simple portions of truth to deceive is an artisan of damage." - Criss Jami

Deceptiveness is defined as the act of hiding the truth, specifically to gain a benefit. This might look like manipulation, but there is a distinct difference. Deceptiveness is often used in the act of manipulation and is one of the many layers in a manipulators scheme. The goal of deceptiveness is to trick and fool the other party. While manipulation is much deeper than that, it does not negate the unfavorable impacts of deception. A lie might take a long time before it is uncovered; however, when it is, the damage and destruction it leaves behind in its wake can be devastating.

I understand the story of a man who had been married for over 25 years. That marital relationship produced three kids between the ages of 11 and 17. All was rosy for the family. The kids went to the best schools, enjoyed the luxuries of life, thanks to the wealth acquired through years of severe and durability on the part of the man. He spoiled his children by making sure that whatever it is they needed, he provided. And who could blame him? For the very first seven years of their marital relationship, the couple was not able to bring forth. They looked for the help of professionals, spiritualists, and even attempted a few unorthodox practices all to no avail. At a point in the marital relationship, when things were at an all-time low, his wife got pregnant. He was thrilled. When the couple added two more kids to the family, it felt as though things could not get any better; but they did.

His wealth grew significantly, and the timing was perfect. One day, the couple got a call that their firstborn had an accident. A lifesaving operation that involved the donation of an organ was required. In the process of contributing his organ to preserve his child, he got to discover the awful secret his wife had kept for several years. The kid was not his. None of the kids were his. Broken, hurt, and ashamed, he took his own life but not without cutting off his wife and kids from his wealth. This deception started as a lie from a single person, but at the end of the day, five people (consisting of the deceiver) were affected. Not to mention the discomfort that would be experienced by the extended family, friends, and colleagues.

In another circumstance, a young start-up firm hired the services of an accounting professional to manage their financial affairs. The owner of the start-up quickly grew keen on this young accountant. It was a strictly organization relationship, but there was a sense of relationship there too. As the company grew and expanded its operations, the business owner turned the majority of the administrative responsibilities to the accounting profession. He showed qualified and was turned over with more responsibilities. These duties added many advantages and perks, and for a while, things were looking excellent. But when a failed deal prompted a quick check on the company's records, the owner was not prepared for the discovery that unfolded. Over the years, he and his business had been systematically robbed to the point where the business's accounts were in the red. The accounting professional fled, and he was delegated to clean up. Within months, the company folded up. Forty-three individuals lost their jobs, and the organization owner lost all his investment and his ability to trust.

The crude thing about deception is that it is built on the real feeling that is essential for the human relationship trust. For an act of fraud to work, a relationship needs to be developed between the victim and the deceiver. The higher the trust, the higher the betrayal. And when there is a deep betrayal, the damaging impact typically goes beyond both people included.

Deception isn't always something that is done to others. Sometimes, it is the lies we tell ourselves. We validate specific actions with the deep lies we tell ourselves. Much like manipulation, lying is also something that everyone does. Some of us may have developed certain ethical principles that make it difficult for us to tell blatant lies or relate to people who do so. It doesn't stop us from telling lies, albeit "little" lies. Understanding the answer to a question but choosing to reject the knowledge of it in a quote to preserve one's social grace is a lie.

Let me explain, let's say you witnessed your manager toss your co-worker's job [something that they worked hard for] in the trash, and you listened as they talked thoroughly on how dreadful he or she believes the concept is. You hum and ham, and when you leave the office, only to be faced by the said co-worker who asks about the boss' ideas on the job. Telling the truth in this instance would do more harm than good. Therefore, you lie. Your intention to trick your associate was for their good.

In dark psychology, the intent to deceive presents more advantages to the deceiver than it does to the victim. As pointed out previously, manipulators use deception to strengthen their hang on their victims. For deceivers, the trick gives an opening into developing a relationship with the victim. The objective is to exploit this relationship for their advantages. One of the most current forms of deception employed today is deceptive affection. People are claiming to feel more love or feeling for you than they do. There are few things that one can use to describe the feeling of being told that someone loves you. This is explicitly rewarding for people who have craved this experience. The deceiver gets the advantages of declaring this false affection in the form of trust, sex, and cash.

Types of Deception

Deception is a type of communication that relies on omissions and depends on order to persuade the subject of the world that best fits the subject. Because there is interaction included, there will be several different types of deceptiveness that could be happening. According to the Interpersonal Deception Theory, there are five various kinds of deceptiveness that are found. Some of these have been shown in the other kinds of mind control, revealing that there can be some overlapping. The five primary forms of deception include:

Lies: this is when the agent comprises details or offers info that is different from the truth. They will present this information to the subject as fact, and the subject will see it as if it the truth. This can be harmful because the subject will not know that they are fed with wrong information; if the subject knew the info was false, they would not likely be speaking with no deception, and the agent would occur.

Equivocations: this is when the representative makes inconsistent, unclear, or indirect declarations. This is done to lead the based on get baffled and not to understand what is going on. If the person comes back later and tries to blame them for the false information, it can also help the agent to note their face.

Concealments: this is among the most common types of deception that are used. Concealments are when the agent leaves out information that is appropriate or important to the context, purposefully, or they participate in any behavior that would conceal information that is appropriate to the subject for that particular context. The agent will not have straight lied to the subject, but they will make sure that the vital details that are needed are not disclosed to the subject.

Exaggeration: this is when the representative will overemphasize a truth or extend the fact a bit to turn the story to how they would like. While the agent might not be directly lying to the subject, they are going to make the circumstance look like a more significant offer than it is, or they may change the fact a bit so that the subject will do what they want.

Understatements: an understatement is the exact opposite of the exaggeration tool in which the agent will minimize or minimize aspects of the fact. They will say the subject that an occasion is not that huge of offer when, in reality, it could be the essential things that identify if the subject gets to finish or gets that big promotion. The representative will be able to go back later and say how they did not realize how big the offer was, leaving them to look good and the subject to look nearly petty if they complain.

These are just a few of the kinds of deceptiveness that might be found. The agent of deceptiveness is going to use any technique at their disposal to get to their last objective, just like what happens in the other types of mind control. If they can reach their goal using another approach against the subject, then they are going to do it, so the list above is in no other way exclusive. The agent of deception can be genuinely harmful because the subject will not be able to say what the reality is and what an act of lying is; the agent will be so competent at what they do that it will be almost difficult to determine the truth and what is not.

Motives for Deception

Scientists have figured out that three primary motives exist in deceptiveness found in close relationships. These would consist of partner-focused motives, self-focused motives, and relationship-focused motives.

-Let's look at the partner-focused motives. In this kind of motive, the agent is going to use deception to avoid causing damage to the subject or their partner. They may also use the deceptiveness to safeguard the subject's relationship with an outside third party, to avoid having the subject fret about something, or to keep the self-confidence of the subject intact. Often, this kind of inspiration for deception will be deemed relationally beneficial, along with socially courteous.

This type of fraud is not as wrong as the others. If the agent finds out something terrible that the subject's friend said about them, the representative may choose to keep it to themselves. While this is a kind of deception, it helps the subject keep that friendship while avoiding the subject from feeling bad for themselves. This is the form of deceptiveness that is found the most in relationships and might also not trigger that much damage if found out. A lot of couples would choose to use this type of deceptiveness to secure their partner.

-Next is the self-focused intention of deception. This one is not considered to be as noble as the very first one and is for that reason, more looked down on than the other methods. Instead of fretting about the subject and how they are feeling, the agent is going to just think about how they feel and about their self-image. In this motive, the representative is using the deceptiveness to protect or enhance their self-image. This form of deception is used to shield the representative from criticism, anger, or shame.

When this deceptiveness is used in the relationship, it is usually viewed to be a more severe issue and transgression than what is found with the partner-focused deception. That's because the agent is choosing to act in a selfish way rather than working to secure the relationship or the other partner.

-Finally, the relationship-focused motive of deceptiveness. This deception will be used by the agent in the hope of limiting any harm that might come to the relationship merely by avoiding relational injury and conflict. Depending on the situation, this kind of deception will, in some cases, help because it is going to make things more complicated, relationship. At other times, it may be the cause of harming the relationship. If you pick to conceal how you are feeling about dinner because you don't want to get into trouble, this may help the relationship. On the other hand, if you had an affair and chose to keep this information to yourself, it is only going to make things more complicated at the end.

Despite the intent of deceptiveness in the relationship, it is not recommended. The agent is keeping details that might be important to the subject; once the subject discovers it, they will begin to lose confidence in the agent and ask what else the agent is concealing from them. The subject is not going to be too worried for a reason behind the deception; they will just be upset that something has been avoided, and the relationship will begin to have a fracture. It is better to stick to the policy of sincerity in the relationship and surround yourself with people who do not practice deception in your social group.

Identifying Deception

If the subject has an interest in preventing deceptiveness in their life to avoid the mind video games that add it, it is always good to learn how to discover when deceptiveness is going on. Often, it is tough for the subject to figure out whether deception is happening unless the agent mistakes and tells a lie that is obvious or blatant, or they oppose something that the subject currently knows to be true. While it might be tough for the representative to deceive the subject for a long time, it is something that will frequently happen in everyday life between people who know each other. Because there are not indeed any

51

indications that are dependable to tell when deception happens, spotting when deception occurs is frequently challenging.

Deceptiveness is capable of putting a big load on the cognitive functioning of the agent because they will find out how to recall all the declarations they have made to the subject for the story to remains credible and consistent. One slip up, and the subject will be able to say that something is not. The representative is most likely to leakage out details to tip off the subject either through verbal or nonverbal cues because of the stress of keeping the story straight.

Scientists think that locating deception is a cognitive process, fluid, and complex and which will often depend on the message that is being exchanged. According to the Interpersonal Deception Theory, deceptiveness is a dynamic and iterative process of influence between the representative, who works to manipulate the information on how they want it so that it's different from the fact, and the subject, who will then attempt to find out if the message is real or not. The agent's actions are going to be interrelated to the steps that the subject takes after they receive the message. During this exchange, the agent is going to expose the spoken and nonverbal information that will hint the subject to the deceit. At some points, the subject might have the ability to tell that the agent has been lying to them.

When the agent is deceptive, it is not always possible to tell. According to Alert Vrij, a kept in mind deceptiveness scholar; there are not any nonverbal habits that are connected with deception uniquely; while some nonverbal habits can be correlated with the act of deceptiveness. These hints can also happen when other behaviors are present, so it is difficult to identify if the agent is using deceptiveness unless they do an outright lie.

Another scholar of deceptiveness, Mark Frank, proposes another idea of deception that consists of how it can be spotted at the subject's cognitive level. When deceptiveness happens, it requires a conscious habit that is deliberate on the part of the representative so listening to words and paying attention to the body movement that is going on are both important when attempting to determine if someone is tricking you. If someone gives up a question and the agent is not ready to address it straight, instead of using some kind of disturbance, has a wrong structure of reasoning, repeats words a lot, and uses less time talking for that particular concern, they are lying.

Mostly, there are not many signs that can be considered when attempting to figure out when deceptiveness is happening. Some nonverbal signs may be present when somebody is deceiving, but they may also have some other problems such as nervousness or being shy.

Main Components of Deception

While it might be hard to determine which aspects show when deception is taking place, some components are typical of deceptiveness. Typically the subject will not realize that these elements have happened unless the agent has informed a straight-out lie or been caught in the act of deceiving. If the representative is using the process of deceptiveness in an ideal way, these are components that will be known as times goes on. The three primary components of deception consist of camouflage, disguise, and simulation.

Camouflage

The first component of deceptiveness is camouflage. This is when the agent is working to hide the fact in another way so that the subject will not know they are missing the information. When the agent uses half-truths when they are disclosing information, frequently, this method will be used. When these facts are revealed in some way, the subject will not know that camouflaging has happened until later. The agent will be knowledgeable in hiding the truth so that it is difficult for the subject to see the deceptiveness by chance.

Camouflage is another component that can be found in the process of deceptiveness. When this happens, the agent is working to create an impression of being something or somebody else. This is when the agent is hiding something about themselves from the subject, such as their genuine name, what they do for a living, which they have been with, and what they are up to when they go out; this goes beyond changing the attire that somebody uses in a motion picture or a play; when the disguise is used in the process of deceptiveness, the agent is trying to change their entire personality to manipulate and trick the subject.

Numerous examples can show using disguise in the process of deceptiveness. The first is about the agent disguising themselves, generally as another person, so that they are not recognizable. The representative might do this to get back into a crowd of people that do not like them, change their characters to make somebody like them, or for another reason to enhance their objectives. Sometimes, the word camouflage can describe the agent disguising the real nature of a proposal in the hopes of hiding an impact or motivation that is out of favor with that proposition. Often this form of camouflage is discovered in propaganda or political spin.

Because it is, camouflage can be harmful, hiding the true nature of what is going on. If the agent is concealing who they are from the subject, it can be difficult for the subject to determine who they are. When info is withheld from the subject, it clouds how they can think, given that they do not have the best information to make logical choices. While the subject might believe that they are making reasonable choices of their own free choice, the agent has taken away crucial info that may change the subject's mind.

Simulation

The third part of deceptiveness is referred to as simulation. This consists of showing the false subject info. Three strategies that can be used in simulation are: fabrication, mimicry, and interruption.

In mimicry or the copying of another model, the agent will be automatically depicting something comparable to themselves. They may have an idea that looks like another person's, and instead of giving credit, they will say that it is all theirs. This type of simulation can typically take place through auditory, visual, and other ways.

Fabrication is another tool that the agent may use when using deceptiveness.

What this implies is that the representative will take something that is found in truth and change it so that it is different. They may narrate that did not include or happen in embellishments that make it sound better or even worse than it was. While the core of the story might be real, yes they did get a bad grade on a test, it is going to have some new things put in such as the instructor provided a lousy grade on function. The reality is that the agent didn't study, and that is why they got a bad grade in the first place.

Diversion is another type of simulation in deception. When the agent attempts to get the subject, they focus their attention on something asides the truth, usually by baiting or using something that might be more appealing than the fact that is being hidden. For instance, if the husband is cheating and thinks the wife is beginning to find out, he might bring home a diamond ring to distract her from the problem for a while. The issue with this strategy is that it often does not last long and the agent needs to look for another method to trick the subject to keep the process going.

Research study on Deception

Deception has become a massive part of everyday life. Whether the agent means to trigger damage or not, there are many instances where deception will creep into relationships of all sorts. The agent may trick their manager into getting more time to finish a job; a spouse may trick their partner in order not to harm their feelings. While many cases are not to trigger harm, they are still present in society. Because of this occurrence, there has been researched done to determine why it happens and who may likely carry out the acts.

Social Research

Socially there has been some research done to see the results of deceptiveness on society. There are several approaches found in social research, such as in psychology, which deal directly with deceptiveness. In these methodologies, the researchers are going to purposefully misinform or mislead their people in regards to what is truly going on in the experiment. This keeps the subjects uninformed as to what is going on and will assist in delivering better results.

A study that was performed in 1963 by Stanley Milgram demonstrates how deceptiveness will work on people.

The agents informed the subjects that they would be helping out in a research study that handled learning and memory; in truth, this research study was looking at how willing the subjects were to comply with commands of somebody who is in charge, even when obedient indicated that they would have to cause discomfort on the other subjects. While the individual who was getting the pain was simply a star and did not indeed get damaged in the experiment, it was found that the subjects would cause the highest readily available discomfort on the actor if informed to do so by the authority. At the end of this research study, the subjects were told what the study's real nature was, and people were offered help to ensure they left in a state of wellness.

Making use of deception in this function has raised a lot of issues with research study ethics. Presently it is being controlled by the American Psychological Association and other expert bodies to make sure that the subjects are being treated relatively and are not receiving undo the damage in the process.

Psychological Research

The psychological research study is the branch that will use deceptiveness the most because this is needed to identify the outcomes. The reasoning behind this deception states is that humans are very conscious of how they appear to others and themselves, as well as the self-consciousness they feel, may misshape or interfere with the way the subject would behave in regular situations beyond doing the research study where they would not feel inspected. The deception is meant to make the subjects feel more at ease so that the agent can get more precise outcomes.

For instance, the agent might be interested in finding out what conditions may make a student cheat on a test. It is not that the subjects would if the representative asks the student outright confess to cheating, and there would be no way for the agent to determine who is telling the truth and who is not. In this case, the representative would need to use interruption to get a precise idea of how typically cheating happens. The agent may rather say the study is to find out how user-friendly the subject is; the subject might even be told during the process that they might have the opportunity to look at somebody else's answers before they give their own. At the end of this deception research, the agent must tell the subject what the real nature of the study is and why the deceptiveness was needed. Also, the majority of agents will offer a quick summary of the results that happened between the participants when the research study is done.

Although deception is used a lot in these kinds of research studies, they are bound by the ethical guidelines set out by the American Psychological Association; there are some disputes about whether deceptiveness is something that ought to be allowed at all. Some think that allowing deceptiveness is not essential, and it is triggering harm to the subjects which are taking part. Others believe that the outcomes would be manipulated if the subjects knew the precise nature of the research study ahead of time. Typically the most significant concern with using deceptiveness in a research study is not the real deception itself. Instead, it is the unpleasant treatment that is used in a research study of this type and the ramifications of what is going to happen in the unwanted research study. This is usually the underlying reason why some are against using this kind of research study and why it is considered to be dishonest.

Another argument against the principles of using deception in these kinds of studies is that the subject has offered their informed grant to participate in the research study. They have read the rules and policies that go along with the research and seem like they are notified enough about the results that are expected to sign a waiver to start. It is argued that if the agent is tricking the subject and excluding essential information about the research study, regardless, it remains in the best interest of the study. The subject is not informed to start. The subject must not be getting involved in the research study because they did not provide consent to the actual research study being carried out because of this.

No matter the arguments that are out there on this subject, there have been some interesting findings when the subjects are tricked about the nature of the study.

For example, in concerns to the research study discussed above (about cheating); if the subjects had been outlined the true nature of the study, it is not likely that many of them wouldn't have cheated because none of them would want to be seen as corrupt or dishonest to others around them.

The deceptiveness allowed the researchers to see what would happen in a real-life application. Besides, if the subjects of the memory test mentioned previously in this book understood the true nature of that study, they wouldn't have listened to the authority figure and administer the outcomes they did.

Despite the objections that have been formed about using deceptiveness in a research study, using deceptiveness has offered researchers a lot of exciting results. These outcomes might not have been possible without the use of deception, considering that the subject may have responded in a different method to the research study.

Approach

Psychology might be the main reason why deceptiveness is used in research, but there is a lot of deceptiveness that has appeared in a modern-day approach. A deception is a routine event in approach. For example, in the meditations of Descartes that were released in 1641, the concept of Deus deception was introduced; this concept was something that could trick the ego, when it believed logically about what was going on in reality. This idea went on to be used as part of his hyperbolic doubt; this is where the subject begins to question everything that is given to the agent because they have been deceived in the past.

Frequently, theoretical arguments will utilize this Deus deception as their mainstay to put in doubt or question the understanding of truth that somebody holds. The first part of the discussion states that whatever the subject understands might be wrong because it is easy to deceive the subject.

This is simply one of the cases of deception found in philosophy. Many works have been composed on this subject, trying to explain what it is, how it affects the subject, and methods that the subject can avoid coming in contact with it. There has also been a great deal of research study done, attempting to figure out when deception might be good and when it can be dangerous. This is for considerable dispute; some people believe that all lying is wrong, while others see deceptiveness to conserve someone's feelings as beautiful sometimes, such as a partner with holding the reality that somebody said something wrong about their wife.

CHAPTER SEVEN

Key Areas In Our Lives That Make Us Vulnerable To Dark Psychology

"Those that go around looking for love just manifest their lovelessness.

And the loveless never find love.

Only the caring find love.

And they never need to seek for it"

- D. H. Lawrence

Now that we have gotten the gruesome part of dark psychology out of the way, let us bring things closer to the house. Let's face it because you check out all that is thought to yourself, hey this does not apply to me; I can never remain in that situation. Granted, the chances of things getting that gruesome are rather slim. Never make the mistake of assuming you are immune to the powers of dark psychology. Its influence is much closer to you than you think. The most common place where elements of dark psychology are manifest is in our love relationships with our spouse.

Love is a universal language. It is a primordial feeling that we all intuitively yearn for. As people, we are created for love. We wish to feel and enjoy love. No one is as happy as a man or a woman who is in love and knows they are loved in return.

Some people befriend for procreation purposes. Some people date to negate social pressure. Some even date to promote the alliance between powerful families. But, the main factor for relationships, aka getting a date, is love. That said, it is easy for things to deteriorate to a point where love is used as a bargaining chip for more power over another person. And this is where elements of dark psychology concerning play.

You have heard of the saying, "use what you have to get what you need". In the company world that type of thinking features the terrain. But in relationships, it is called a manipulation. Let's explore this example; a woman knows that her partner discovers her tempting and sexually attractive. Possibly there has been something she wanted from him for a very long time but has failed to obtain his willingness to comply regardless of the long drawn out discussions they might have had. Let's say that what she has always desired from him is his substantial contribution in doing your house chores.

His obstinate position prompts her to device a way to make her partner end up being certified. She has to do this without coming to him outright and saying something like "arrange the living-room; otherwise, there will be no sex tonight." That has been understood to happen in particular homes, and it would backfire, especially if you are dealing with people who have a natural dislike for taking directions from others no matter how well it is phrased. Instead, she bids her time. She pounces on him when she discovers him in the middle of doing a random chore. Giving him sweet awards and saying things like how she finds him so appealing when he is doing [anything she sees him doing] and after that, she indulges his sexual craving for him.

The effect of this strategy is even higher if he usually has to "work" to get her this thrilled. If she does this consistently, he subconsciously picks the message that him doing house chores might equal him having great sex later. Gradually, he ends up being set to doing the chores he would naturally have declined to do since of the sexual inspiration his partner deals with.

This circumstance is seemingly harmless. But if you observe, dark psychology was utilized here. The man was manipulated into doing things, albeit voluntarily for his partner just for sex. She understood his weak point and played it to her strength to get what she wants. The good idea is that in this case, everybody is happy. Because the woman receives the valuable contribution she needs from her partner, and the man gets the sex he longs for with the woman he wants. Things are not always this mutually advantageous when dark psychology is involved. This can get dark for the victim.

Let us look at this other couple.

I would call this new couple Dave and Maya. Dave and Maya have contrasting personalities. Dave is a house friend, and Maya is a lively extrovert with many good friends. On the surface, it would appear that their difference in characters matched each other perfectly. This was until Dave felt the need to exercise more control over Maya. However, he understands (probably because he has currently attempted) that he can't use straight-out force to get what he wants. He begins a project to get Maya under his thumb. He starts by not picking little information about her like her choice in clothing, makeup, hair, and even makes snide remarks about her weight under the guise of love.

This begins to affect her confidence, and when she brings up her good friends, he uses lightweight occurrences to back and show up his theory about some fictional feud between them [things like they are envious of you works] These little seeds of doubts grow and blossom into a wedge that drives Maya and her good friends apart. Without any good friends and wrong esteem concerns thanks to her new-found low self-confidence, she is made to seem like Dave is the only person who cares about her and accepts her for who she is. This drives her to wish to do everything she can to please Dave, thus putting her where he wants her to be under his thumb and totally under his control.

In the two cases I used, as an illustration, we see instances where relationships that are supposed to be about the two persons ends up being a channel to meet the desires of one partner through manipulation and deceptiveness. Both relationships started with reasonable objectives, and while completion outcome of the previously shown to be an acceptable circumstance for both parties, in the later story, the reverse is the case. The similarities here are all victims did what they did out of their loves for their partners. It, therefore, goes on to say that our desires to be enjoyed can leave us vulnerable. It can be controlled and exploited for the gains of others.

Blind Faith And Religious Beliefs

"If we seek solace in the prisons of the distant past Security in human systems we're told will always always last. Emotions are the sail and blind faith is the mast without the breath of real freedom we're getting nowhere fast." - Sting

I am going to throw this out there and state that blind faith does not just refer to the belief in one supreme God or higher deity. Some people chose to think about science. Despite what religion you practice, there is a reality that our faith often develops a blind area that distorts the truth, causing us to make choices that we would not if we are in our right and the proper frame of mind. However, before we get into the why, let us take a look at the why.

When I discussed vulnerability in an earlier chapter, I said that the last things that make us human are some of the things that make us vulnerable and prone to the machinations of dark psychology. For some people, these impacts appear than others. Our beliefs in divine beings precede even the earliest civilization. Man has always regarded his existence as a small portion in the universal scheme of things; therefore, we think that there are forces that are bigger, higher, and divine. This kind of thinking made sense because it helped our minds cope with the difficult things that happen around us if you examined things logically.

You see a beautiful flower and admire how something so elegant and delicate might just be without an idea, without a pattern, it is. We take a look at the big expanse of the sky and wonder what lies beyond.

Does it just go on permanently?

Or does it merely tapper off into an unlimited end?

When you hear the mighty roar of the waterfall or the earth-shaking sounds made by a thunder blast, even with the improvements and understanding provided to us, we still quake in worry and awe. At that time, your options were to let the fear drive you insane, or you rationalize the circumstance by pinning it on a sovereign being that is bigger than you. A few of the braver folk picked to use science to do their explanation.

Sticking with this same line of thinking, when someone we enjoy dies, we are needed to challenge our mortality. Our sorrow is intensified by concerns relating to life and death. Does the journey end here, or does it continue to lifetime? This has been a strong motivational force behind today's belief systems. The fear and consideration provided to the life after this life has stimulated many into making the "right choices" here so that when death comes, the life that we hope continues after us agrees for us. It is our way of controlling the final result, so to speak because the choice as it is represented to us is so grim. Some people prey on our fear of the afterlife that they use it to manipulate us into getting what they want.

If we hold this afterlife theory in such high esteem, you can think of how we treat people who are considered mouthpieces of the deities that control the afterlife. Pastors, Imams, Rabbis, and all other kinds of religious leaders are held in such high reverence that their words are considered the expressions of the divine being in question. Generally speaking, these spiritual leaders are meant to use ethically sound principles under their respective offices and act in the best interest of their members. If not for any other reason, at least to promote the tenets of the faith they declare to represent. However, this is not always the case, as we have pertained to recognize. A lot of spiritual leaders abuse their functions and impact by deceiving their members into making choices that only serve their selfish interests.

The typical tactic is to use the name of the first divine being to twists the words that are drawn from the faith's sacred book to mean new things that prove whatever story they are making up to assist them in manipulating people effectively. A lot of people have been duped, physically harmed, and even made to dedicate god awful crimes under this guise. Another approach these wrong leaders use is claiming to have a vision or spiritual insight into a particular need that the victim has. They develop an intricate story that is a mishmash of lies interspersed with the fact (generally acquired unknowingly from the victim or third party), and the main objective is to extort the victim for money, favor or power play.

Some victims are persuaded to part with more money than they can ever hope to have. In many cases, young impressionable victims are persuaded into living in worry under occult like situations.

But, situations like these don't end in spiritual houses. Some people are not connected with any religion, but they like to consider themselves spiritually open. Such people would encounter phony psychics and mediums who claim to have a strong connection with the netherworld. Again, our attachment to death and our concerns for what happens after death clouds our judgments and leaves us open to scoundrels who want to control the situation to their advantage. They use the same trick of the wrong religious leaders using deceptiveness and lies to control their victims. Victims choose a 10-minute psychic reading of their horoscopes and palms only to get strung along for years with pledges, modified realities, and false hopes, causing them to spend thousands of dollars browsing for the elusive "reality."

People who position their belief in science are not unsusceptible to manipulations. If you believe that because your faith is anchored to legible and factual science, you can not be influenced, think again.

People revert to what they believe in when there is a crisis. For a science believer, you naturally turn to science. There are cases where people with debilitating medical conditions seek out nontraditional medication in a quote to outlast the illness. Understanding that the best standard medicines have failed, they turn to these outliers who claim to have the option with their experimental drugs and not done before medical treatments. Sadly, these processes are too dangerous, too pricey, and typically uninsured. However, the slim chance of life is worth every penny, and this is what the fraudulent people exploit.

And it is not in crisis. You have people come up with ideal solutions to a big problem like weight reduction and so on. They claim that their most current diet fad, question tablet, or innovation can change us using scientific theories that have not been evaluated and verified. A lot of people buy into the guarantee of this transformation based on info that has been mainly controlled to extort victims. The primary distinction between spiritual con leaders and these purveyors of fake science is that instead of a deity, they use science when scamming their victims. And sadly, the majority of people do not understand till is far too late how they are being affected.

Those who use dark psychology key into your deepest needs and exploit it when it comes to belief. They use that which you hold spiritual to control your idea process. And often, the sacredness of it doesn't truly matter. As long as it is essential to you, they consider it a cash cow of some kind. When that person is experiencing a crisis, and there is no higher time to mine and private so to speak than in your minute of crisis, you are at your weakest and most vulnerable to the influences of people and others have been known to manipulate things to benefit.

Social Conditioning

"Where justice is denied, where poverty is implemented, Where ignorance prevails and where anybody class is made to feel the society is an organized conspiracy to oppress, rob and deteriorate them, neither persons nor property will be safe."
- Frederick Douglas

At a seminar back when I was in school, I heard an argument where somebody vehemently said that we are a product of our society. Because I was fortunate to know many successful people who defied their community and distinguished themselves by achieving very remarkable tasks, I desired to dispute that right there. As I grew older and experienced more about life, it occurred to me that these individuals were the "exceptionals". It is an undeniable fact that the society we live in plays a remarkable role that forms us in more ways than we can imagine. The ugly truth is that the way we believe, live, and work can be traced to the influences of our society, and these are some of the essential things that dark psychology exploits.

Social conditioning refers to the impact that society has on your life as a whole. While social conditioning looks more at your social status in terms of earnings, living conditions, and so on, its reach can go deeper than that. Your society can and does influence your beliefs and religious beliefs. You may not be a direct practitioner of those beliefs, but you are indirectly impacted by it. In some cultures, some days are considered sacred. That means, conducting service on those days may be thought-about an offense. However, seeing as we have simply discussed faith in the previous chapter, let us take a look at other aspects of social conditioning that can easily be influenced by dark psychology.

There is a fundamental misconception that being part of a society that is advanced makes you resistant to the impacts of culture. And I get that type of reasoning. How can something as ridiculous as culture impact a society that gave birth to the likes of Albert Einstein and Neil Armstrong? Well, you are wrong on that count. If anything, you are more vulnerable, and I will tell you about it in a bit.

The most significant development our society has made today remains in the place of innovation. We reside in a world where things are performed in a flash. Cash transactions are completed at the press of a button. A business person can conclude a handle China, inspire his group in South America, talk to his partner through a crisis at home and give an impressive marketing pitch in Dubai all before the morning is done just by pressing some buttons. This is the world we live in today. If you are coming up with a company strategy in this era, your services and products have to match the same speed that we are all used, or else you are setting yourself up to fail. And this is great. Because I am relatively sure that no one missed the grand old days when it took one entire month to get a mail from across the country or three puffs of black smoke shooting up in the sky to tell you that your dear likes you back. No. We appreciate the pace with which things are done these days.

Unfortunately, this speed that defines our daily lives makes us vulnerable to get costly fast plans. We hear all these remarkable stories of people who ended up being millionaires overnight, and on some subconscious level, we want the same thing. Some people have exploited these desires to their advantage with what we now called Ponzi schemes. Named after the notorious Charles Ponzi, a Ponzi scheme is a diabolical way of bringing out daytime break-in with full permission from the victim. The scammer creates a fictitious enterprise that guarantees significant ROIs. After the victim makes a preliminary dedication, he is rewarded with "returns," which attract him further into the trap the perpetrators have set out, causing him to put in more funds. To even maximize his revenues, the victim is controlled into having more good friends to make investments. The more good friends he brings, the higher his returns. This builds pyramid investors, all putting their funds into this business that does not exist. In truth, what the fraudsters are doing is merely robbing Peter to pay Paul. And then they pay themselves too. This continues till one day, the business just vanishes into thin air, leaving lots of victims stranded and without their initial financial investment or interests on it.

The only sensible description we can give for a situation like this where a business with hardly any registered documentation of its presence is available in and rip-offs tough working people who are typically smart in their dealings is social conditioning. It occurred in the 1800s in the 1900s and it is still happening till today. And despite the understanding of its existence, people are again falling for Ponzi plans. It like we are simply configured to do it. And it is not merely restricted to a particular class of people. Both rich and people poor fall for it. That tells us that the wrongdoer victims on something that these two classes of people have in common, which is a desire to make more cash and to make that money quick.

It does not end there. To successfully devote this crime, they rely on our sense of neighborhood. You are most likely to patronize the services or items of business if you were offered a direct referral by somebody you trust that the recommendations of a random stranger. If your sister says she made Xyz quantity of cash on financial investment and she shows you evidence of it, intuitively, your trust triggers you to base your choice practically totally on their reference. And when you get your payment, you automatically end up being an ambassador for the brand. This makes you spread your news to other people in your network, and the link continues. This is an extremely human habit, and a lot of manipulators would take advantage of this. As soon as they get what they need, they disappear or get taken in by their greed and get caught.

You may argue that this situation is not most likely to happen to you because you are simply too wise for this so, let me bring it closer to you using technology that we go to bed with and wake up to another day. The social network is the fad of our time. People have become "overnight" feelings thanks to social media platforms like YouTube, Instagram, Twitter, and Facebook, among others. This has triggered some of us to nurse comparable dreams; however, until that happens, we want to know for the likes and comments we get. The issue is that our natural desire to get in touch with people can end up being somewhat obsessive if the focus is on our virtual relationships on social networks. This grows into a difficult idea process where one's sense of achievement is equated with the variety of likes, follows, and comments one can get from a post.

People who start thinking like this stop paying attention to their actual real-life relationships. Instead, they lead pompous and fake lives so that they can get approval that, in an unfortunate way, verifies their daily lives. In their mission for importance, they starve themselves emotionally and subject themselves to the unapproved and sometimes vicious opinions of others. This kind of habit has been linked to the boost of self-destructive behavior in people who use social networks. Paradoxically, social media, which was designed to help us get in touch with other people and construct our network, has broken lots of people due to its dark impacts.

Ambition And Personal Aspirations

"High aspiration is the passion of a great character.

Those endowed with it might carry out extremely bad or great acts.

All depends on the concepts which direct them."

- Napoleon Bonaparte

All of us have an order of business. Often, this list is simply a group of tasks developed to assist us in making it through the day. And often, it is a roadmap to where we wish to be in the nearest future.

Example: Your grocery shopping list gets you through the day because you can get what you need to make dinner and possibly the standard essentials that help you become a better member of the society (ye old regular bathing soap keeps the bad smells away and the society thanks you for it).

Are you drawing up an organization strategy for your start-up? That is a different ballgame. You are want to set yourself up for the future financially and quite possibly, giving a product or service that affects the lives of people favorably. In today's terms, we call that "boss moves." Aspiration is what drives you towards those goals you set for yourself.

Do you desire something? You press yourself to achieve it, and for the more enthusiastic folks, when they reach their goals, they merely push themselves more.

Aspiration is an appealing quality in any human.

The goal to be better than who, what, and where you are now and frequently putting you at the wheel that guides your life; no one wants to be with people who are content to sit on the sofa throughout the day doing nothing more than eating potato chip and watching the television. People wish to be with someone who is delighted about the stunning future they picture for themselves and are carefully working to accomplish it. As appealing as aspiration is, when it is put in overdrive, it can bring in the wrong set of people into your life since it leaves you open and vulnerable. Because ambitious people are explained as anything but sensitive, this might sound like a contradictive statement. However, as you will concern discover in this book, what you allow to consume, you gain manage over you, and when you have no control, you end up being vulnerable. In earlier chapters, I spoke about how predators use the weak points of their victims against them. Bearing this in mind, you would agree that aspiration is an admirable quality in a person, and as a strength, it can assist you in navigating your path to success. As a weak point, it can very quickly be the designer of your destruction.

Ambition is more concrete in its desires, while aspirations are those honorable notions that we nurse to make us feel better about ourselves. On their own, neither ambition nor goals need to bring you harm, but when other elements come into play, they can be used to control and trick you.

Many companies believe that ambition is one of the superior qualities of a potential employee. And this is because ambitious people are more ready to do what needs to be done to advance the company than their more seemingly docile counterparts.

People like these are incredibly focused and have a one-track mind when it comes to bringing out their obligations, often offering no idea to what it would take to do it even if it would suggest stepping on the toes of some associates.

An individual who does not rule in their ambition can be convinced and controlled into doing things that are ethically and ethically wrong so that they can satisfy their objectives. It is people with lofty aspirations and goals that are most likely to fall for manipulative techniques that include blackmail. For example, a young professional man with a sterling track record and a high position within a business is most likely to do anything to keep that status quo if he is enthusiastic. Even if those things he is expected to do would further taint his credibility if the understanding of those deeds ever emerged. This is not to say that the rest of the people are less likely to become victims of blackmail and other forms of manipulation. Control is not about physically wielding a vast, dangerous axe over an individual to force them to do something that they would not normally do. It is a game of subterfuge and deception. The manipulator imitates a mirror that captures the desires, aspirations, and aspirations of the victim and, after that, threatens the actualization of that vision by showing the victim's weak point.

The victims made to wrongly believe that their only hope of restoring their dreams is to abide by the ideas of the manipulator. The more powerful the ambition, the most likely the victim will comply, especially if they are convinced that they can get away with doing it.

The acts they might be manipulated into bringing could be anything from weakening the authority figure in their lives, committing an act that may be offending, or among any of whatever else the manipulator might have in mind. Let me scale this back to relatable proportions. In all our relationships with people, there is a process of trust. No matter how paranoid you maybe, even the organization relationship you have with your tailor is a sign of some level of confidence in that you are trusting them to assist you to cover your nakedness without getting hurt while doing so. In as much as there is trust, there is likewise mistrust. But we strive to overcome these feelings in the hope of preserving the bond/bridge between the people included.

At best, we want to maintain civility with those around us. A predator with destructive intent can expound on the distrust by sowing seeds of discord to help them get the results that they desire, which could be your commitment or that of your equivalent or even both.

 Little incidents are blown out of tensions, and percentages are escalated while doing so. Ultimately, the relationship is broken down beyond repair. The allegations hurt you on one end and the counter allegations injure your peer. Neither of you recognizes that a third party benefited from the emotional aspirations for each other (and yes, there is such a thing) and controlled you into the existing state you are.

This goes on to say that our aspirations and aspirations are not always about the product things that we desire. It is also shown in our perceptions and expectations from the relationships in our lives. Dark psychology is used by the predators amongst us to change this perception and manipulate it to their advantage.

Psychological Scars

"It has been said, "time heals all wounds."

I do not concur. The injuries stay.

In time, the mind, safeguarding its sanity, covers them with scar tissue, and the discomfort decreases, but it is never gone."

- Rose Fitzgerald Kennedy

One of the most substantial residual results of every experience we have his feelings, they say that in life, the experience is the best teacher. Let me share one of my most memorable experiences from journeys in recent times.

When there was constant laughter or concern explicitly directed at me, my translator occasionally chimed in, but for many parts, I just observed. And that was when I saw in this kid for not more than eight or nine months, I believe. I can't tell you at that age only that the kid was crawling towards the fire. I took a look around the fire, but no one seemed to be paying any attention. So, I made a relocation to intercept the kid; however, I was immediately reprimanded. All the interpreter told me that the child was about to find out a valuable lesson. I was concerned. The fire pit wasn't blazing hot, but some of the wood still had the fire on them, and cinders were lying about that was still glowing. I enjoyed the acutely.

The kid interested in the little flames crawled better and then stopped. Possibly the heat from the fire had offered him a pause. But, then, the brave lad decided to proceed and brave the heat. He paused at a safe range and then held out his hand towards the flame, which he quickly withdrew. His face registered a shocked expression, and I might see his lower lip trembling. I wished to go to him; however, the man beside me should have noticed my objectives because he signified me to wait. The bad baby's expression moved from injured to among confusion. It was like he was telepathically talking to the flame and asking why it harmed. He tried using his hand again, and this time he wept. The guys laughed and cheered. A woman, rather potentially his mom who must have been standing extremely nearby, quickly stroked in and carried him away.

It is called experience. He went on to assure me that no one would allow anything harmful to happen to the child; but, I get the feeling that his definition of dangerous is far different from what I picture it to be. There are lessons in life that just experience can teach you, and each encounter leaves an emotional scar.

There are particular experiences in life that would quickly induce the never once again reaction from us. What I have described here is the body's response to fear; however, worry is not the only emotion that can be set off by your experiences. There is an extended-spectrum of feelings varying from anger to zealousness that can be set off by an experience.

A woman in love memorizes her enthusiast fragrance. And whenever she gets a whiff of that fragrance, her mood is changed. Sometimes, it causes pleasure, and on particular occasions, it can trigger desire. If that relationship evacuates, the scents might induce unhappiness or rage, depending on how bad the break up was. All I am saying is that emotions belong to the human experience. We act in a specific way when we feel a particular way. Individual events can set off feelings that cause us to respond unusually. My near-drowning experience as a teenager triggers me to worry anytime I close my eyes under a shower. These reactions are set off by the emotional scars we bring. Now, let me discuss the science of this.

When anything occurs, whether good or bad, your brain determines that event with a specific feeling. If this was your experience), this would describe why something as simple as the smell of newly baked bread can transport you to your childhood. (A great deal of marketing companies and ad agencies employ this knowledge in their marketing technique. They attempt to know their item with experiences, events, or things they understand the appeal to you or other people like you (their target demography). Subconsciously, your brain identifies those activities or experiences with their services or products. To sell an outdoor grill, they don't say and come, "hi, here is our remarkable outdoor grill. Buy it". Instead, they feed you with images of a fun 4th of July family yard cookout. You would see kids running around happily, smiling grandparents talking up some relative and the teenagers doing something cool. All of these sprinkled with a good beef cut simmering on the grill. It is as if they are saying if you buy this grill, you also buy into this experience. Simply put, you were aesthetically controlled into purchasing.

This is not necessarily ominous per se. The routine individuals we satisfy in our everyday lives can prey on this weakness. If you are quickly emotionally triggered, you can be controlled into making rash decisions on anything from impulse purchase to succumbing to people on psychological principles alone.

People can disguise themselves and make themselves into something they are not. They wear clothing and fragrances that make it look as if they are rich, and because you have a secure psychological connection with wealth, you look beyond other warning signs and make a regretful choice. Whether bad or good, your psychological scars can make you susceptible to deception and adjustment.

CHAPTER EIGHT

How to Break Free and Accept that You Have a Problem

"Many times, it's not about being a brand-new person, however ending up being the person you were to be and currently are, however, don't know how to be." - Heath L. Buckmaster

A lot of times, we stay more on the viewpoint of others. Of how the world sees us or how we desire the world to see us. The lifestyle pattern of this present age has its slogan, "phony it up until you make it." This sort of approach to living causes us to have a loose and quick relationship with the truth. We are so caught up in fabricating that we are not able to manage the mask even when we are alone with ourselves. This type of self-deception can implant itself deeply in our lives that we may wake up one day and find ourselves in a situation that opposes the phony truth we have worked so hard to protect and often shocks us to our extremely core. If we are to be sincere, we are not captured continuously off guard by the lies that we are told. On some level, we understand. What makes us off guard is just

95

how much we are injured by it. And it is this hurt that makes us avoid the issue in the first place. To break free, the first action is confronting the situation and breaking off any impressions. You can not go again if you do not shatter the perceptions that surround you. Arm yourself with the knowledge that you have an option. Make the conscious choice to see things for what it is. That offer that appears too excellent to be true might be great to be real.

Next, trust your gut instincts. There are times that a lie has been so masterfully made that it appears to be true. In times like that, it is easy just to dismiss those feelings and go with what you are being told.

These are tiny circumstances and may not lead to big payoffs. Still, it builds your self-confidence in your impulses so that when situations of real consequence develop, you can discern what your desires are saying and act on them. If you are currently in a circumstance and don't have the time to train your ability to trust your instincts, you need not to lose hope. In this situation, you simply want to get out of it.

That question would lead you to this next step. Ask the right questions. Start with yourself. Attempt to find out why you feel the way you do. Take a look at your present scenario, figure out why you are no longer content with the way you feel. Ask yourself why you feel the way you do and see if you can be more specific about your feelings. I said that feelings make you susceptible; however, they can also act as a guide when you feel lost. When you are unable to provide the answers adequately, you look for, look outside yourself. Looking outsides yourself does not necessarily mean you should confront the predator, although it may eventually get to this. I don't recommend going the direct route instantly as you will offer the wrongdoer an opportunity to provide a defence that may cloud your judgment the more and not get you the results you prefer. It can also clue the person that you might be on to them. This may trigger their battle or flight action. Instead, have people within your cycle of trust. Given that you are presently trying to navigate through a situation that includes a breach of trust, it may be hard to select who to trust unexpectedly. If you are worried about that, then go to someone who has little or no personal stake in the formula. Someone who is not directly related to you or the person(s) involved may be best. These people are most likely to be sincere with you.

When you ask the questions, the next essential thing is to listen to the answers. This might sound somehow incredulous because, duh, you are going to be listening to the responses. The reality is that our self-deception can trigger us to be selective about the reactions we get. We tell ourselves we are listening; however, we are just genuinely paying attention to the responses we want to hear instead of the answers we are getting. You might have shattered the illusions around you; however, there is still a part of you that clings to the comfort that those illusions bring.

The discomfort of challenging the reality of the situation would prevent you from hearing the genuine responses to the questions you have asked.

Actual listening needs some sense of detachment, but not from the truth this time around. You need to remove yourself from your emotions.

Your detachment from your emotions would lead you to the next step, which is processing the new details logically.

Performing illogically can complicate situations more than they already are.

Letting all the emotions simmer and spring up to the surface makes your exit way that much tough. When faced with the fact which might simply allow everything goes to hell, the illogical part of you. Your anger, which is righteously warranted, can spur you to take actions that help calm your emotions in the short term. But in the long run, you might concern regret those actions. I am not saying you need to reject your feelings; I am saying you should not act based on those feelings. Handle the circumstances initially and then your emotions later on.

Act Quickly

"It's the action, not the fruit of the work that is necessary.

You have to do the right thing.

It may not be in your power, may not be in your time that there will be any fruit. That does not mean you should stop doing the best thing.

You may not know what results originated from your action.

If you do nothing, there will be no outcome. "

- Mahatma Gandhi

You have confronted the reality of your scenario, and that is the hardest part. You can not hope that the situation would just go away on its own. Something as simple as notifying your close pal of the reality of the case can set a series of occasions that will ultimately set you free.

After making the option to act, you must understand that the fabric of impression is made out of a harder material than glass. When your feelings are in high gear, the illusion might be working its way back into your heart by using pieces of your emotions to fix it.

The person they use may not remain in league with them. They are probably just manipulated into doing the things they do. Liars have no problems using friends, family, and even religious leaders to get what they want. You need to defend the choice you have made and make up your mind to see it through.

When the tactic to manipulate you through other people stops working, the next thing they do is resort to their old method, which is leeching on to your emotions. In divorce scenarios, spouses use their partner's emotional issues for their child to drag them down. Hazards like if you leave, you are never going to see the kids again are used. In service dealings, there is generally a suggested danger to cut the other person off with no type of payment. This is a desperate effort by the manipulator to attempt to manage their victim. They know that their chars are no longer efficient and feeling threatened by their loss of control; they use power plays like trying to get the upper hand. Power plays generally includes kinds of blackmail, ranging from minor things to deep secrets that were turned over to them when the relationship was good. The blackmailer may desire to get financial payouts, take more advantage of in the settlement deal, and for the more sinister people, they just want control.

At this point, their actions might have you in a corner, making you want to snap and react. I highly advise against this. If you're going to get out of this unscathed, you will need both your logic and your impulses. Although the fact of the scenario is that when you discover you have been consistently lied to, you end up being mentally scarred so, the question of leaving the situation unharmed ends up being mute. Priority needs to be given to take the route that enables you to move away from that harmful situation without further damaging yourself. Mentally, you are all over the place. Rage, disappointment, hurt, and anger are simply the tip of the iceberg. But you need to think realistically. Keep your head above water and be alert.

They say that an animal is more unsafe when it feels cornered. For a man, it is worse. When an individual has been caught in the web of deceit that they wove themselves, they want to do everything to safeguard themselves. Then, their selfish impulses to keep themselves protected kicks into overdrive, and they are willing to do anything to avoid facing the effects of their actions. As with human nature, it is not possible to forecast the degree they are eager to go to prevent this. Rather than wave your plan to bring them to justice in their face, your concern should be making sure that you are safe. I would recommend a physical separation even if it is short-term from the person who you feel is manipulating you if it is possible. Not only does this help in giving you room to think clearly, but it can also assist in compromising the hold that they have over you. If they are in their area can make you more vulnerable to more manipulations because staying the same proximity.

Don't fall for it as this could be another ploy and another act to control you into taking less extreme measures that they may not be helpful. If you feel your resolve weakening is getting out.

Get Help Fast

"The best way to not feel hopeless is to get up and do something.

102

Don't wait for the advantages to come to you.

If you go out and make some good ideas, you will fill the world with hope, and you will fill yourself with hope." - Barack Obama

When you find yourself trapped by the adjustments of others, among the feelings you will experience is confusion. This contributes to clouding your cognitive thinking leaving with a sense of vulnerability. At this moment, you may even be questioning the reality of what you are doing. It will lead to rejection if you continue to amuse these doubts. You will likely want to conclude that you have gotten the entire situation wrong. It will be as if you came and misinterpreted specific things to the wrong conclusion. This type of thinking would drive right back to the arms of the manipulator. Resist the desire to offer in by getting a second opinion. In a health crisis, people go to another physician to get a second viewpoint. This is to get rid of any iota of doubt you might have about the first medical diagnosis and verify the best course of treatment for you. In the same way, getting the viewpoint of another person can help you discern the reality of the situation and what your next actions might be. Just keep in mind, it is much better to go to somebody who has proven many times that they have your helper.

Now that you have the confirmation you need, do not try to take on the obstacle on your own. The situation may not be something you want anybody other than yourself to know. Now, your concern is coming out of the scenario and enduring it enough to prosper no idea what it would take to walk in your shoes. Reach out for it and be ready to accept it if you need the extra bit of assistance. By all means, please do if you can deal with the circumstance yourself. Just be sure that every decision you take, the goal is to get you out and not get you into other people's conditions. You should have more than that.

If the perpetrator exists in the cyber world, you would have to involve the police and pertinent authorities, especially if the individual deceived you of your money. Look for hints to the person's true personality in the conversations you have had, and only when you are equipped with sufficient evidence to confront them. Of course, with the authorities included, you would still get them ultimately. It might take longer than it usually would if you had patiently prepared yourself before doing the confrontation.

If you fear for our life in any way, please do not challenge this person on your own. Inform the people who care about you and have at least somebody present during this meeting. If you are in an abusive situation, this is what I would encourage you to do;

1. Reach out to a regional company that caters to victims of abuse in your area. This is most likely the best and essential action to take as they have professionals who are there to assist you and counsel you on your next plan

2. Get out while you can. Do not wait on that big pay, the best moment, or some important event. When you get the opportunity, take it and use it. Deal with the aftermath later on. And if the prospect does not present itself, have a safety plan that would lead to your escape. Do all you can to stay alive, and as soon as the moment emerges, cease it.

After confronting the criminal and taking the necessary steps to leave the situation, you need to start the recovery process without delay. It doesn't matter the scale and gravity to which you were hurt, controlled, or abused. You need to move past it and wait for some time. "heal", your injuries need more than resting on your couch and reliving the past. Time would give you an adequate distance from your experience, but if you have discovered anything from this book, it is the reality psychological scars never recover in most cases. If you do refrain from doing something about it, an unhealthy scab might form over the wound, leaving you merely as susceptible if not more than when you were living the experience. Talk with a counselor, go to therapy, whatever you chose to do, take an active role in helping with the healing process. It will not happen overnight; however, you are sure that with each day and each action you take in therapy, you are closer to improving.

CHAPTER NINE

Brainwashings

Some who believe in the power of brainwashing think that people around them are trying to control their minds and their habits. For the many parts, the process of persuasion happens in a much more subtle way. It does not involve the ominous practices that many people associate with it into many more detail about what brainwashing is and how it can influence the subject's way of thinking.

What is Brainwashing?

Brainwashing in this book will be discussed in terms of its use in psychology. In this relation, brainwashing is described as a technique of idea reform through social impact. This type of social influence is happening during the day to everyone, regardless of whether they recognize it or not. Social impact is the collection of methods that are used to change other people's behaviors, attitudes, and beliefs. For example, compliance methods that are used in the office might technically be thought about a form of brainwashing because they need you to act, and when you are doing the job, you feel a specific way.

Brainwashing can end up being more of a social problem in severe form because these methods work at changing the way somebody thinks without the subject's approval.

For persuading to work effectively, the subject is going to go through total seclusion and dependency because of its intrusive impact on the subject. This is one of the reasons that some of the brainwashing cases that are understood, happen in totalistic cults or jail camps. The brainwasher, or the agent, need to gain complete control.

This means that they should control the eating practices, sleeping patterns, and fulfilling the other human needs of the subject, and none of these actions can happen without the will of the agent. Throughout this process, the representative will work to systematically break down the subject's whole personality to make it not work right anymore permanently.

The method of brainwashing is still up for dispute, whether it will work. A lot of psychologists hold the belief that it is possible to brainwash somebody as long as the right conditions are present. Even then, the entire process is not as extreme as it is presented in the media. There are likewise different meanings of brainwashing that make it harder to figure out the effects of brainwashing on the subject. A few of these meanings needs to be some threat to the physical body of the subject, to consider brainwashing. Even the practices done by lots of extremist cults would not be regarded as fact brainwashing as no physical abuse happens if you follow this definition.

Other definitions of brainwashing will count on control and browbeating without physical force to get the change in the beliefs of the subjects. In any case, experts think that the effect of brainwashing, even under the perfect conditions, is just a brief term occurrence. They believe that the old personality of the subject is not removed with the practice; instead, it is put into hiding and will return when the new personality is not strengthened anymore.

Robert Jay Lifton created some intriguing ideas on brainwashing in the 1950s after he studied detainees of the Chinese and Korean War camps. During his observations, he identified.

This process started with attacks on the sense of self with the prisoner and then ended with an expected change in beliefs of the subject.

There are some steps that Lifton defined for the brainwashing process in the subjects that he studied.

1. An attack on the personality of the subject

2. Requiring regret on the subject

3. Forcing the subject into self-betrayal

4. Reaching a breaking point

5. Providing the subject leniency if they change.

6. Funneling the guilt in the intended direction

7. Launching the subject of supposed guilt

8. Progressing to consistency

This indicates that all of the normal social references that the subject is used to coming in contact with are not available. Also, mind clouding strategies will be used to accelerate the procedure, such as poor nutrition and sleep deprivation.

Be real of all brainwashing cases; typically there is a presence of some physical damage, which contributes to the target having problems in thinking independently and seriously like they usually would.

Brainwashing is the first type of mind control to be considered. Brainwashing is the process where somebody will be connived to abandon beliefs that they had in the past o take new perfects and worths. There are many manner ins which this can be done, although not all of them will be considered harmful. For instance, if you are from an African nation and after that relocate to America, you will often be needed to change your worths and suitable to harmonize the brand-new culture and environments that you are. On the other hand, those in prisoner-of-war camps or when a new totalitarian federal government is taking over, they will often go through the process of brainwashing to encourage citizens to follow along quietly.

Lots of people have mistaken beliefs about what brainwashing is. For some part, the practice of brainwashing will land somewhere in the middle of these two concepts.

During the practice of brainwashing, the subject will be persuaded to change their beliefs about something through a combination of various techniques. As the subject absorbs this new info, they will be rewarded for expressing concepts and thoughts which go along with these originalities. The fulfilling is what will be used to strengthen the brainwashing that is happening.

Brainwashing is not new to the society. People have been using these methods for a very long time. For example, in a historical context, those who were detainees of wars were typically broken down before being encouraged to changes sides. Some of the most compelling cases of these would result in the detainee becoming an impassioned change to the new team. These practices were new at the beginning and would typically be implemented depending on who supervised. Over time, regard to brainwashing was established, and some more methods were presented to make the practice more universal. The newer strategies would depend on the field of psychology because many of those ideas were used to show how people might change their minds through persuasion.

Many steps go along with the brainwashing process. Off one of the main requirements that come with brainwashing being successful is that the subject should be kept in isolation.

The subject can be around other people and affects, they will find out how to think as a person, and the brainwashing will not work at all.

When the subject is in isolation, they will go through a process that is meant to break down theirself. After months of going through all this, the subject will feel like they are bad, and the guilt is going to overwhelm them is desired. The subject will be led to think that the new options are all their own and so it is more likely to stick.

The entire process of brainwashing can take some months to even years. It is not something that is going to happen in merely a conversation, and for some parts, it will not be able to occur beyond jail camps and a couple of separated cases. For some parts, those who undergo brainwashing have done so when someone is simply attempting to convince them of a new perspective. If you are in an argument with a friend and they encourage you that their concepts make sense, you have technically gone through brainwashing. Sure, it might not be wicked, and you were able to think of it all realistically, but you were still convinced to change the beliefs that you held previously. Unusually, someone goes through real brainwashing where they will have their whole value system replaced. It will generally take place during the process of coming around to a new viewpoint, regardless of whether the techniques used were persuasive or not.

Kinds Of Brainwashing

- **Breaking Down of Self**

During this process, the agent desires to break up the old personality of the subject to make them feel more susceptible and open to the preferred new status. The agent is not going to be successful with their intention if the subject is still firmly set in their willpower and their old personality. Breaking up this personality and making the person question the things around them can make it easier to change the personality in the later steps consisting of an attack on the personality of the subject, bringing on guilt, self-betrayal, and then reaching the snapping point.

- **Attack on personality**

The assault on the personality of the subject is the systematic attack on the subjects' sense of self-esteem, their ego or personality, and their core system of belief. The agent will spend a lot of time rejecting everything that the subject is guarding. "You are not a man!" "You are not a fighter!" The subject will be under attacks like these continuously for days and months. This is done to weaken the subjects so that they end up being disoriented, baffled, and exhausted. When the subject reaches this state, their beliefs will start to look less intense, and they might begin to believe the things that they are told.

- **Guilt**

Once the subject has gone through the attack on their personality, they will get to the stage of regret. The subjects will be continually told that they are bad while going through this new personality crisis.

The subject will always be under attack for something they have done, regardless of how huge or small the acts is. The range of the attacks can vary as well; the subject might be criticized for their belief systems to the way that they dress and because they eat too slowly. Over time, the subject is beginning to feel embarrassed around them all the time, and they will feel that all the things they are doing are wrong.

- **Self-betrayal**

Now that the subject has been led to believe that they are bad and that all of their actions are unfavorable, the representative is going to work to force the subject to admit that they are bad. At this moment, the subject is drowning in their own regret and feeling extremely disoriented. Through the continuance of the mental attacks, the threat of some fantastic physical harm, or a mix of the 2, the representative will be able to require the subject to knock his old personality. This can consist of a wide range of things such as getting the subject to denounce their peers, friends, and family who share the same belief

While this process may take a while to occur, once it does, the subject will feel like he betrayed those that he should be faithful to. This will also increase the pity and the loss of personality that the target is already feeling, and break down the character of the subject the more.

By this point, the subject is feeling broken down and disoriented. The subject is in a personality crisis at this point and is going through some profound embarrassment because they have betrayed all his beliefs and the people that he has understood; this will make the subject go through a nervous breakdown.

The subject may have the feeling of being completely lost and having a loose grip on truth. As soon as the subject reaches this breaking point, they will have lost their sense of self, and the representative will pretty much be able to do everything they want with them at this point considering that the subject has lost their understanding of what is going on around them and who they are.

At this point, the representative will set up temptations that are necessary to convert the subject towards a new belief system. The new system will be set up in a manner to give redemption to the subject from the torment that they are feeling.

- **Possibility of Salvation**

After the agent has been reliable at breaking down the personality of the subject, it is time to move on to the next action. This action involves giving the subject to the possibility of salvation only if they follow their belief.

The subjects are allowed to know what is around them, they are told that they would be good again and that they would feel better if they would simply follow the brand-new preferred path. Four steps are consisted of in this phase of the brainwashing procedure; leniency, a compulsion to confession, transporting of the regret and releasing of the grief.

Tolerance is the "I can help you" stage. The subject has been broken down and needed to turn away from the people.

The subject is going to feel lost and all alone in the world, disgraceful of all the bad things that they have done and wondered which way they can turn to. When they reach this phase, the representative can provide them some type of release used to help them.

This will typically remain in the type of a reprieve from the abuse the subject has incurred or some other small kindness. The agent can use a little additional food or a cup of water to the subject or even take a few moments to ask the personal subject questions about the family and loved ones. In the subject's present state, these little acts of kindness will look like a big deal, leading to the subject feeling a great sense of gratitude and relief towards the agent. Often these feelings are escape of percentage in contrast to the offering that has been made. In some cases, the subject might feel like the agent has done the act of conserving their life rather than use a small service. This distortion of events operates in favor of the agent as the subject will get ties of loyalty with the agent rather than distant memories.

- **Compulsion to Confession**

Once the representative has been able to get the trust of their subject, they will try to get a confession out of the process. If the brainwashing process is efficient, the subject might even begin to feel a desire to reciprocate some of the compassion that has been used to them by the agent.

Confession as possible ways to alleviating the subject of the discomfort and guilt that they are feeling; the subject will then be led through a process of confessing all the wrongs and sins that they have committed in the past.

Naturally, these wrongs and sins will be about how they impact the brand-new personality that is being developed. For instance, if the subject is a detainee of war, this action will allow them to confess the wrongs that they did by defending freedom or fighting against the routine of the other country. Even if these are not always sins or wrongs, they break the new ideology that the regime is still best and so they must be confessed.

- **Carrying of Guilt**

As soon as the subject enters the channelling of guilt step, they have been going through the assault of their self for some months. By the time the subject reaches this point of the brainwashing process, they will feel the regret and shame that has been put on them, but it has lost its significance. They are unable to inform you precisely what they have done wrong to make them feel relieved; they know that they are wrong.

The agent will be able to use the blank slate of the subject to describe why they are in pain.

The representative will have the ability to connect the sense of guilt that the subject is feeling to whatever they want. If the representative is trying to replace a system of beliefs, they will take the old system and encourage the subject that those beliefs are what is making them feel regret.

This is the stage where the agreement between the old beliefs and the new beliefs are established; generally, the old belief system has been developed to correspond with the psychological misery that the subject has been feeling while the new belief system has been established to refer the ability to leave that pain. The choice will be the subjects, but it is pretty easy to see that they would pick the new system to start feeling better.

- **Releasing of Guilt**

In this action, the subject has come to realize that their old worths and beliefs are causing them pain. By now, they are used down and tired of feeling the guilt and embarrassment that was put on them for some months. They start to realize that it is not always something that they have done that makes them feel that way; but, it is their beliefs that are causing the guilt. The embattled subject can feel some relief from the truth that there is something that they can do about it.

The subject has found out that they have a way of escape merely by leaving the wrong belief system that they have held and welcoming the available new one. All that the subject needs to do is to launch the guilt that they are feeling is to denounce the institutions and people that are associated with the old belief system; and, they will be launched from the regret.

The subject now has some control over this stage. They will be able to understand that the release of guilt is up to them entirely. All that the subject needs to do for this stage in breaking free from wrongness is to confess to the dedicated relation of the old belief system. As soon as the full confession is made, the subject will have finished the complete psychological rejection of their former personality. The representative will need to act at this moment to give a brand-new personality to the subject and help them to rebuild their character into the preferred one.

- **Rebuilding of Self**

By this step, the subject has gone through a lot of actions and psychological turmoil. Once all this has been reached, the subject will need to know how to rebuild himself, with the help of the agent.

The subject is a clean slate and is very eager to learn how to be and feel better, two steps are seen during this phase consisting of harmony and the final confession before starting over.

Harmony

The agent will use this action to persuade the subject that it is their choice to make a change. They may tell the subject that they have the option to pick what is excellent and make a change that will help them to feel better.

Stage, the representative will stop the abuse and instead make a point of giving the subject mental patient and physical comfort. The point of doing this is to align the old beliefs with the discomfort and suffering while lining up the brand-new ideas with happiness and relief.

This stage is established so that the subject is given the option of the road to take, even when it doesn't depend on them. The subject needs to use this stage to pick between the old beliefs and the new beliefs, effectively identifying how they are going to feel for the rest of their lives. By this point, the subject has already gone through the process of denouncing their old belief.

Because of this, they are likely going to choose the new system of belief to alleviate their regret. Using reasoning and considering the state of mind that the subject is, it is easier to see that the only personality that the subject is going to choose for their peace of mind and security is the new one.

- **Last Confession and Starting Over**

Although the choice is not theirs at all, the agent has tactically worked the entire consistently to lead the subject to look like they have the freedom to choose the brand-new personality. If the brainwashing process is done correctly, the subject will think logically about the new options and determine that the best one is to use the original personality. They have been conditioned to believe by doing this, and in their unique mindset, it is the one that makes one of the most sense. There are no other options; picking the brand-new personality allows them to be free from the guilt and causes joy while choosing the old nature, which results in pain and regret.

If, for some reason, the subject denies the brand-new personality, there would be backtracking in the entire brainwashing process, and they would be forced to undergo it all once again to wind up with the desired outcomes.

124

During this phase of the process, the subject gets to choose that they will pick good, which implies that they get to decide to go with the brand-new personality. When the subject contrasts the misery and pain of their old nature with the peacefulness that comes with the brand-new, they are going to choose the brand-new personality.

Offer with regret and unhappiness any longer. As this stage completes, the subject is going to decline their old nature and will go through a process of promising allegiance to their brand-new one, knowing that it is going to work at making their life much better.

Sometimes, some ceremonies and routines take place during this last. The conversion from the old personality to the brand-new nature is a big offer because much energy and time have been used on both sides. During these events, the subject will be inducted into the new neighborhood and embraced with a unique personality. For some brainwashing victims, there is a feeling of rebirth during this period. You are allowed to embrace your new nature and are welcomed with open arms into the new neighborhood that is now your own. Instead of being separated and alone, you have many brand-new friends and neighborhood members on your side. Instead of feeling the guilt and pain that has afflicted you for many months, you are going to feel joy and peacefulness with everything around you. The brand-new personality is now yours, and the brainwashing transformation is total.

This process can happen for many months to even years. The majority of people are set in their personalities and beliefs; it is not possible to change all this in some days unless the person was already going to change which would make the brainwashing methods unnecessary. Isolation would also be needed because outside influences will prevent the subject from relying on the representative during this process. This is the reason why many brainwashing cases happen in prison camps and other separated circumstances; the vast bulk of people will not have the chance of coming across brainwashing because they are always surrounded by people and innovation that would impede the whole brainwashing process. As soon as the person remains isolated, the process takes a very long time because many steps that need to be taken to change the ideals held by the person for several years for them to accept the brand-new personality as their own while feeling that the option has been continuously theirs as well.

As can be seen, there are a few steps that should be taken to go through the brainwashing process. It is not something that is going to happen just by running into someone on the street and exchanging some words.

Trying to dislodge a confession that the subject is terrible and they wish to renounce all the things that they have done that are bad due to their old personality. Finally, the subject will be led in the direction of thinking that they can change for the better if they simply desert their old ideas and welcome the tranquillity and rightness that surrounds the new personality that is available. All these actions need to happen for the brainwashing to be efficient and the latest nature to be put in place.

Persuading as Court Defence

During history, people have been claiming that they committed dreadful wrongs since they had been induced. Whatever the action was, brainwashing was a simple defence because it took the responsibility of the action away from the accused, and it was difficult to prove whether someone had been persuaded or not.

Whether persuading pleas can be used as a defence in the courtroom depends on some dispute. Many experts feel that by allowing this defence into the courtroom, the courts would become overloaded with incorrect claims of brainwashing, and the resources for negating this defence or show would be more than what the courts could deal with. Regardless of this, there are some cases brought to court that might show the credibility of brainwashing as a defence for crimes committed.

The first example of this happened in 1976. Patty Hearst, the heiress to a big publishing fortune, used the protection of brainwashing when she stood trial for a bank robbery. In the early 1970s, Hearst was abducted by the SLA, the Symbionese Liberation Army, and ended up joining this group. During the trial, Hearst reported that she had been locked up in a closet for some days after she had been abducted. While in the closet, Hearst mentioned that she hesitated of her life, brutalized, tired, and was not fed. At the same time, members of the SLA bombarded her with their ideology against a capitalist nation. Within the two months of her kidnapping, Patty had changed her name while giving a declaration saying that her family was "pigHearsts" and then appeared on the security tape of a bank-robbing along with those who had abducted her.

In 1976, Patty Hearst stood trial for this bank break-in and was protected by F. Lee Bailey. In the defence, it was claimed that the SLA had persuaded Hearst. This brainwashing had required Hearst to devote a criminal activity that she wouldn't have done under any other circumstances. In the mindset that she was under with the brainwashing, she was not able to discriminate between ideal and wrong and, therefore, need not be found guilty of the bank robbery. The court did not agree with this analysis and instead found her guilty and put her in prison for seven years. After some years, President Carter changed her sentence, so she just ended up spending two years in prison.

CHAPTER TEN

Manipulation

Brainwashing and hypnosis are the two forms of mind control that quickly enter your mind. While these two are essential to comprehending the functioning of mind control and how all of it works, they are not the only readily available options. Others can be used and are typically more efficient in the short-term than either brainwashing or hypnosis. These particular strategies are ones that can be used in everyday scenarios, for example, like in regular conversations a person may have with others. While it is not most likely that a person will be manipulated or convinced to change major beliefs through typical discussions, they can be persuaded to change little things such as being encouraged to acquire cookies from a regional woman scout or to vote a specific way in an election.

The main thing to keep in mind about the following three forms of mind control is that they are most likely to take place in an individuals' everyday life with the people that they know and trust. An individual is not going to put their subject into seclusion or require them into a changed frame of mind as with brainwashing. Instead, they will use different strategies to change the way their subject thinks.

The three types of mind control that suit this category consist of power, deceptiveness, and persuasion.

This chapter is going to go over adjustment and how it can work to change the way "the subject" thinks. While alignment may not put the person who is employing the strategy in danger or cause any immediate threat.

It is established to work deceptively and questionably to change the behavior, viewpoint, and perception that the designated subject has in question to a particular subject or situation.

What is Manipulation?

In this book, we will talk about control in terms of psychological manipulation, which is a social influence that works to change the habits or understanding of others, or the subject, through violent, misleading, or questionable methods. The manipulator is going to work to advance their interests, generally, at the expense of others, so many of their techniques would be considered deceptive, devious, violent, and exploitative.

Social influence, such as when it comes to a medical professional working to persuade their patients to start adopting healthy routines, is usually perceived to be something safe. This is true of any social impact that is capable of appreciating the right of those included to choose and is not unduly coercive. On the other hand, if somebody is trying to get their way and is using people against their will, the social impact can be damaging and is generally towered above.

Emotional or mental manipulation is seen as a kind of persuasion and coercion. Some parts are in this type of mind control, such as bullying and brainwashing. For the many components, individuals will see this as misleading or abusive.

Those who decide to use control will do so to manage the habits of those around them. The manipulator will have some objective in mind and will work through various abuse kinds to coerce those around them into helping the manipulator get to the last goal. Frequently emotional blackmail will be involved.

Those who practice control will use mind control, brainwashing, or bullying techniques to get others to complete the jobs for them. The subject of the manipulator may not wish to carry out the task; however, they feel that they have no other option because of the blackmail or different technique used. The majority of people who are manipulative, absence the proper caring and sensitivity towards others, so they might not see an issue with their actions.

Other manipulators just want to get to their final goal and are not concerned with who has been bothered or hurt along the way.

Also, manipulative people are typically scared to enter into a healthy relationship because they think others will decline them. Somebody who has a manipulative personality will frequently have the inability to take responsibility for their behaviors, problems, and life. Considering that they are unable to take the blame for these concerns, the manipulator will use the methods of adjustment to get another person to take control of the responsibility.

Manipulators are frequently able to use the same strategies that are discovered in other forms of mind control to get the impact they want over others. Among the most commonly used methods is known as emotional blackmail. This is where the manipulator will work to inspire compassion or guilt in the subject they are manipulating. These two emotions are chosen because they are considered the two highest of all human feelings and are the most likely to stimulate others into the action that the manipulator wants. The manipulator will then have the ability to take full benefit of the subject, using the sympathy or regret that they have developed to persuade others into complying or helping them reach their final goal.

Frequently, the manipulator will not just be able to create these feelings; they will have the ability to motivate degrees of sympathy or guilt that are escape of percentage for the situation that is going on. This means that they can take a case such as missing out on a party like the subject is losing out on a funeral or something that is more important.

Emotional blackmail is just one of the tactics that are used by manipulators. Another way that have been successful for many manipulators is to use an abuse that is called crazy-making. This technique is typically aimed at the hope of producing insecurity in the subject being manipulated; frequently, this self-doubt will.

At times, the manipulator will use types of passive-aggressive habits to bring about crazy-making. If the manipulator is caught in the act, they will use rejection, reason, rationalization, and deceptiveness of ill intent to get out of the difficulty.

One of the most significant concerns with psychological manipulators is that they are not always able to recognize what others around them might need, and they will lose the ability to fulfill or perhaps think about these needs. This does not excuse the behavior that they are doing. Still, frequently the requirements of others are not considered or are not a top priority to the manipulator, so they can perform manipulative jobs without feeling guilt or pity. This can make it hard to discuss and stop the habits in a rational way why the manipulator should stop.

Besides, the manipulator might find that it is challenging for them to form long and significant friendships and relationships because the people they are with will always feel used and will have trouble trusting the manipulator. The problem goes both ways in the development of relationships; the manipulator will not have the ability to recognize the needs of the other individual while the other person will not have the ability to form the needed emotional connections or trust with the manipulator.

Needs to Manipulate Successfully

An active manipulator should have strategies at hand that will make them effective at using people to get to their final objective. While there are several theories on what makes an active manipulator, we will take a look at the three needs that have been set out by George K. Simon, a capable psychology author. According to Simon, the manipulator will need to:

1. Have the ability to conceal their aggressive behaviors and objectives from the subject.

2. Have the ability to figure out the vulnerabilities of their designated subject.

3. Have some level of ruthlessness readily available so that they will not require to deal with any doubts that may develop due to hurting the subjects if it comes to that. This harm can be either psychological or physical.

The first requirement that the manipulator has to achieve:

If the manipulator goes around informing everyone their strategies or always acts mean to others, no one is going to stay long enough to be manipulated. Instead, the manipulator needs to have the ability to conceal their thoughts from others and act like everything is normal. By the time the subject is conscious of the concern, the manipulator has enough details to persuade the subject to continue.

Next, the manipulator will need to have the ability to determine what the vulnerabilities of their intended victim or victims are. This can help them to figure out which tactics need to be used to reach the overall goal. In some cases, the manipulator might be able to do this action through a little bit of observation while other times, they will need to have some kind of interaction with the subject before coming up with the full strategy.

The third requirement is that the manipulator needs to be ruthless.

It is not going to work out if the manipulator puts in all their work and then frets on how the subject is going to fair at the end. It is not most likely that they would be going with this plan at all if they did care about the subject. The manipulator is not going to care about the subject at all and does not care if any damage, either psychological or physical, befalls the subject as long as the general goal is fulfilled.

One reason why manipulators are so capable is that the subject often does not know they are being manipulated until later in the process. They may believe that whatever is going on is fine; possibly, they think they have made a brand-new friend in the manipulator. By the time the subject knows they are being used or no longer wishes to be a part of the process, they are stuck. The manipulator will have the ability to use strategies, including emotional blackmail, to achieve their goal.

CHAPTER ELEVEN

Persuasion

Persuasion is another type of mind control that is going to be discussed. While there might not be as much media buzz about this type of mind control as there, it is with brainwashing and hypnosis, and it can be as effective if done correctly. The concern with this kind is that there are so several types of persuasion that are present in life that it can be difficult for anyone source to get through to the subject and make a distinction.

While persuasion works to change the ideas and the beliefs of the subject like the other types of mind control, it looks like everybody is trying to persuade you about something, so it becomes easier to disregard the persuasion that is coming towards the subject. For example, the commercials on tv, when an argument is going on, and even when a conversation is going on, there is some kind of persuasion that is taking place. People will often use persuasion to their advantage without discovering. This chapter is going to go into more detail about belief and how it can be successfully used as a kind of mind control.

What is Persuasion?

To start with is the definition of persuasion. They will often come up with different answers when people think about persuasion. Some might consider the commercials and advertisements that they see around them that urge the purchase of a specific product over another. Others might think of persuasion in regards to politics and how the candidates might attempt to sway the voters' opinion to get another vote. The two examples above are persuasion because the message is trying to change the way the subject is thinking. Persuasion can be found in daily life, and it's an active force and significant influence on the subject and society. Marketing, mass media, right choices, and politics all will be influenced by how persuasion works, and it will work on convincing the subject too.

As can be seen, there are some crucial distinctions between persuasion and other forms of mind control, which have been discussed earlier in this book.

Brainwashing and hypnosis will need the subject to be in seclusion to change their minds and personality. An adjustment will also deal with just someone to get to the final objective. While persuasion can be done on only one subject to change their mind, it is also possible to use persuasion on a larger scale to persuade a whole group or perhaps society to change the way they think. This can make it more efficient, and possibly unsafe because it can change the minds of many people at once instead of the thought of just a single subject.

Many individuals fall under the misconception that they are immune to the impacts of persuasion. They believe that they would have the ability to see any sales pitch that is tossed their way, whether the agent is actually selling an item or some brand-new concept.

Also, the majority of subjects will be able to avoid the messages about buying TVs and luxurious vehicles or the most recent item in the market. Most times, the act of persuasion is going to be more subtle, and it can be tougher for the subject to form their viewpoints about what they are being told.

When the act of persuasion is brought up, many people are going to see it in an unfavorable light. They will consider a conman or a salesperson who is trying to encourage them to change all their beliefs and who is going to push and bother them till the changes take place. While this is one way to consider persuasion, this procedure can typically be used in a positive way instead of an unfavorable way. For example, public service projects can prompt people to give up smoking or recycle can be kinds of persuasion that can enhance the lives of the subject. It is all in how the process of persuasion is used.

Aspects of Persuasion

Just like the other types of mind control, there are certain aspects to be seen out for when it comes to persuasion. These components help to define what persuasion is so that it is more identifiable. According to Perloff in 2003, persuasion is itemized as "A symbolic process in which interactions attempt to persuade other people to change their behaviors or mindsets concerning a problem through the transmission of a message in an environment of free choice".

This is among the essential things that make persuasion different from the other types of mind control; the subject is often allowed to make their free choices in the matter even if the tactics of persuasion are going to work to shift the subject's mind in a particular direction. The subject can choose which way they wish to believe, if they want to buy an item or not, or if they think the proof behind the persuasion is strong enough to change their minds.

There are a few elements that exist in a persuasion that help to define it even further. These elements include:

Persuasion is symbolic.

This means that it makes use of images, words, and sounds to understand.

Persuasion will involve the agent intentionally trying to influence the subject or group. Self-persuasion is a vital part of this process. The subject is generally not persuaded, and instead, they are given the flexibility to make a choice. There are some manner in which convincing messages can be sent, like face to deal with, television, radio, and web.

The interaction can also occur nonverbally or verbally.

Let's take a look at each of these points in a little more information.

The first aspect of persuasion is that it needs to be symbolic. To encourage somebody to believe or act in a particular way, you need to tell/ show them why they must change their thoughts. This is going to consist of the usage of words, sounds, and images to get the new point throughout. You can use words to launch a dispute or argument to show your point of view.

Pictures are a fantastic way to show the proof that is needed to convince somebody to go one way or another. Some nonverbal hints are possible, but they are not going to be as reliable as using the images and words.

The second key is that persuasion is going to be used intentionally to influence the way others are acting or thinking. This one is quite apparent; if you are not deliberately attempting to influence others, you are not using persuasion to get them to change their perspective.

On the other hand, it could get a lot more involved and consist of more misleading forms to change the subject's mind.

The unique feature of persuasion is that it allows the subject to have some kind of freedom. The subject is allowed to make their own choice in the manner. For the many parts, no matter how tough somebody attempts to persuade them of something, they do not need to go for it. The subject may listen to a thousand commercials about the best car to buy, but if they do not like that brand name or do not need a new car at that time, they are not going to buy it.

If the subject protests abortion, it is not going to matter how many people come out and say how fantastic abortion is, the subject is not going to change their mind. This allows more liberty of option than what is found in other types of mind control, which might tell why many people do not see this as a kind of mind control when asked.

Persuasion is a type of mind control that can take place in different ways. While brainwashing, hypnosis and manipulation have to happen on face to face basis, and in many cases in complete seclusion, persuasion is capable of taking place in other ways. You can see examples of persuasion all over the place including when you are talking to people you know, on the Internet, and through radio and television. It is also possible to give convincing messages through spoken and nonverbal means, although it is far more effective when spoken methods are used.

Modern Persuasion

Gradually, persuasion has been able to change and evolve from its initial beginnings.

There have been quite some changes made to the art of persuasion and how it is used in modern-day times. Some of the vital components of modern-day persuasion will be discussed in this chapter.

Richard M. Perloff has actually spent a fair bit of time studying modern persuasion, how it is used, and how it can affect society as a whole. He composed a book called The Dynamics of Persuasion: Communication and Attitudes in the 21st Century, which outlines the five manners ins which using modern persuasion is various from how it was used in the past. These five ways are:

The number of messages that are thought about convincing has grown by leaps and bounds: In the times of ancient Greece, persuasion was used merely in writing and debates amongst the elites. The incident of persuasion was not a big thing, and you would not see it always. In modern times, it is hard to get anywhere without some message of persuasion.

There are still people knocking on your door trying to get you to purchase something, believe their ideas, or try something new. Persuasion is much more of modern-day life than it has been at any other time in history.

Persuasion travels quickly: back in the times of ancient Greece, it could take weeks or longer for a convincing message to get from one point to another. Many acts of persuasion had to be done in the context of face to face communication.

As soon as in just seconds and any message can be spread easily, political prospects can reach constituents at once. When it is spread out so quickly, persuasion takes much more substantial function.

Persuasion can mean a great deal of money: now that companies have discovered the power of persuasion, they are doing everything they can to make it work for them. The more effective they are at encouraging customers to buy their items, the more money they will make.

Some companies stay in business solely because of the moving process, such as public relations companies, marketing companies, and advertising agencies. Other companies will have the ability to use the persuasive techniques provided by these companies to reach and surpass the sales objectives that they set.

Persuasion has become more subtle than in the past: at the beginning of persuasion, the representative would announce their views out loud for the whole group to hear in the hopes of getting them all to change their minds. Those days are over, and the process of persuasion has ended up being far more discrete. While it is possible to see acts of persuasion that are still extremely loud and in your face, such as in some kinds of advertising, others are following a more subtle path.

An example of this is when organizations craft a particular picture of themselves, such as being family-friendly, to get people's attention.

Regardless of being more subtle, persuasion is still as efficient today as it has ever been. The process of persuasion has become more complicated: and persuasion is more subtle and often harder to figure out; it is also going along the roadway of becoming more complex.

As soon as a person simply went to the one store in town to purchase whatever they require, now they can choose from different shops for their needs from the hardware store to the grocery shop and the clothing store. All these options make it difficult for the agent to find an excellent convincing message for the consumer or any other subject.

CHAPTER TWELVE

Best Ways To Shield Your Defence Against Dark Psychology

Don't Conceal

"It isn't the initial scandal that gets people in this difficult situation; it is trying to cover-up." - Tom Petri

To go through something as attempting and distressing as dealing with lies of somebody you trust can have a profound mental impact. My goal was to help people sieve through the lies in their daily environment and live above the controls of others when I started this book. The entire focus of this book has been 80% on helping look inward and the rest was committed to helping you comprehend what dark psychology is all about. There is one aspect that we never touch and this is something you are going to experience on your own. That element is the people who commit these acts. I offered the necessary information to help you decipher aspects and characteristics of dark psychology, but that is as far as I can go.

This is because people who are most likely to use you and control you are people you have come to like and trust. The period of the relationship you may have had with them does not mean that they are incapable of injuring you. Sometimes, the times spent with you help cement you rely on them, making you more vulnerable and more prone to their charms. That is not to say all the relationships you have would cause some type of adjustment down the line or that strangers unexpectedly pose a lower characteristic. My point is, there is no chance to identify that this person is going to harm you merely. The best you can do is check out for the signs I mentioned and keep an open mind because you might struggle more with the concept that this person you relied on hurt you this way than the real thing that was done to you.

And try not to let your feelings cloud your ability to make reasonable choices. Because being controlled sucks, and people who do it deserve some type of penalty, but we all understand that things are usually more complicated than that. What if the person is your sister, brother, spouse, best friend, spiritual leader?

Next, choose whether their relationship is worth continuing.

Your partner cheating on you and lying about it all this while is terrible, but do you want the act to be the end of that relationship?

I would start by asking, barring the offense they devoted, how was the relationship?

If you chose to quit the relationship, you would need to find out how to manage the relationships that are connected to fall out from this. If there are ties, depending on the nature of the relationship, both of you may have to come together with a narrative on how you want to continue. You can just choose to go your separate ways without giving anyone any additional information as you owe them no explanation if those relationships are unpredictable. Do your best to move and heal without harming any other relationship unless you have to. If you decide to continue with your relationship with the person, you have your work to do because it is going to be a severe, long uphill struggle. You will survive it, no doubt but not without commitment and effort.

Both parties would have to show their determination to heal the relationship. The person who defaulted would have to work hard on restoring your trust. And the person hurt would have to work hard at discovering to believe that person again.

For beginners, you might want to give each other space after the preliminary crisis. Space could be anything from a few days to some weeks, but it ought to not exceed a month. Use this time to process your feelings about the incident. Because as painful as their attempt to separate the person from their action, it may seem like making excuses; however, it isn't. If you have chosen to repair this relationship, you might have to take away this method in your thinking.

Conversations might look suppressed at first, but with time, the man came back to the rhythm. Avoid bringing up the past every time you argue. Clinging to what has happened makes it difficult to grow past it and grow to where you want to be.

Above all, trust that you have made the right choice. Stay rooted in the present and trust that you have made the right and reasonable choice to heal things. Do not heighten the pressure on yourself by making it compulsory that the brand-new relationship must work.

Forgive Yourself

"Take a walk through the garden of forgiveness and pick a flower of forgiveness for anything you have ever done.

When you get to that time, make complete and overall forgiveness of your whole life and smile at the arrangement in your hands because it is lovely."

- Stephen Richards

People assume that when you are wrong, the main party that needs forgiveness is the person that dedicated the offense in the first place. In a situation like this, where a relationship was established with the transgressor, and that transgressor took advantage of the relationship, one of the people who need forgiveness is the victim. There is a reason why even when relationships have been disconnected with the wrongdoer, you still find yourself experiencing feelings like anxiety, anger, irritability, stress and anxiety, mood swings, among other things.

You feel guilty for being gullible, vulnerable, and for usually putting yourself in a situation where you were quickly controlled in the first place. You are feeling guilty about the hurt you think you induced yourself. We have all be in this situation eventually. We feel guilty that either our inactions or actions led to the hurt of others even though we were not directly included in the perpetration of the act. The first thing you need to do is remind yourself that despite what happened, it is not your fault. You may not be able to change this understanding overnight, but over time, by continually advising yourself of this truth, you will start thinking about yourself. To, even more, verify this belief, you also need to advise yourself that the lessons you have gained from this have put you in a better position to secure yourself against any comparable incident from happening in the future.

The next thing is to accept that the past is not something you can change. It has happened, you have learned, and you have proceeded. There is no need to keep reliving the experiences you had. Home on what it is, what may have been, what you might have, ought to have and would have done can not in any way change a single second of what has happened. The best you can do is pick up the lessons you have learned and formed them into the brand-new concepts to live. You have fearlessly accepted the truth of the circumstance despite the lies you were told. Now is the time to accept that this business was concluded in the past, and it remains there. You might be dealing with the aftermath of the crisis; however, that doesn't mean that it is still happening. Take every day as it comes and finds more reasons to look forward instead of looking backward. If you are feeling so nervous about the past, you can get a day to re-enact the past.

One way to do this is by having a psychological re-do. Draw up what you think you could have done to change things giving all that you do know now. And after that, proceed. The function of this workout is to provide you with some kind of control over what has happened.

Reclaim your power and carry on to the next thing.

Now that you have re-written the past, it is time for you to turn over the next page and start the next chapter of your life. Start by tackling your remorses. These have a way of compounding our feelings. Accept that you did the best you could do under the circumstances and give you room to grow. Keep in mind; your case was not a criminal offense. You simply had the misfortune of relying on the wrong people. Appoint the blame to the right person. Using affirmatives like "I constantly fall for the wrong person" or "I am so gullible" is hugely self-limiting.

Dig deeper into yourself to discover exactly where those ideas are coming from.

When you have recognized the underlying feeling, you can move past these negative affirmations. And the longer you accede to these unfavorable expressions; the more severe your anxiety levels are going to get. This is because you may end up being somehow paranoid about your relationships with people, seeing opponents only were friends, and reading the wrong meaning in every action.

Lastly, there is the concern of love. We might be extreme in our transactions with others, but the person we are most severe with is ourselves. We find it easier to forgive the criminal than to forgive ourselves, and the expense of these habits is self-destructive patterns that show up in our other relationships.

We undermine those relationships before they even begin.

Using the guise of avoiding another manipulative relationship, we destroy brand-new relationships. The real reason for these habits is the loss of the feeling of self-love. Deep down within, you don't feel you should love, but because you would rather hear that from yourself, you burn bridges. There are pills to help you cope with anxiety and depression, but there are no tablets to help get to that place where you fall entirely in love with.

There are no hard or fast guidelines on how to start this journey to self-discovery. I believe that waking yourself up daily with favorable affirmations like, "I enjoy myself and I deserve to be enjoyed" is a start.

And when you have resolved your concerns with the past, forgiven yourself, and begun the process of learning to love yourself, it is now time to let go. All that pain to go, all that negativity, all that anger, own it for a moment and then release. All the steps listed in this chapter are fantastic, but the healing process is only completed when you release it.

Trust Your Instincts

"They are typically based on truths submitted away simply listed below the mindful level."

- Dr. Joyce Brothers

I chose to devote time to discuss this in detail because when you are handling the forces of dark psychology, your main defence against it is your instinct. While your brain is interpreting signals based on truths, reasoning, and sometimes experience, your heart is dealing with the opposite end, sieving info through a filter of emotions. Your gut instinct is the only thing picking up vibrations that neither the brain nor the heart can rely on. And if you can groom yourself to that point where you know your inner guide and are trained to react to it, you lower your possibilities of being seduced by people trying to work their manipulative idea on you.

For beginners, recognizing this voice is hard. This is because, in our lives, we have enabled sounds of doubt, self-discrimination, and loud sounds of the critics within and without to hush our authentic voice. This voice or instinct depends on your survival. So, trust that when it starts, it senses things in your immediate area that your brain neurons can process. Some people call it instinct, and some describe it as an impulse, they are undoubtedly the same thing, especially when it comes to relationships. To start trusting your instincts, you need to accept that it may not always make logical sense. If you have ever remained in the middle of doing something and suddenly experienced the feeling of being seen, then you know what I am talking about. You have no eyes at the back of your head; there is nobody else in the room with you; however, you get the tiny shiver that runs down your spine and a "sudden understanding" that you are being viewed. That is what I am saying.

The first action to connect with your instinct is decluttering your mind of the voices that you have let in; that voice that you know is you.

Next, pay attention to your ideas.

Why do you think in a specific way about a particular person? As you explore your ideas, you end up being more attuned with your intuition and know when your instincts kick and how to react to it. If you are the kind of person who chooses to make spur of the moment decisions, you may need to take action back to believe and stop briefly.

To be able to trust your instinct, you have to be open to the concept of trusting yourself and trusting others. Your inability to trust others would just make you paranoid, and when you are paranoid, it is not your instincts that kick. You have to let go of your worry, embrace trust, and let that lead to your brand-new relationships.

Lastly, you need to re-evaluate your priorities. If money and product possessions are at the forefront of your mind, you may not be able to see past them. Every interaction you have with people would be interpreted as people trying to benefit from you, and if you harp on this adequate, it quickly becomes your truth. You understand how you attract what you consider in your life. You will just draw in people who believe the same way as you if you are continuously thinking about material wealth.

Using this as a guide, view all your relationships, the old, the brand-new, and the point of view with this new hindsight. Do not go into a relationship expecting to be played. Whether it is a service relationship, a romantic relationship, and even the routine associate, be open when you approach them. That way, you can get the best feedback from your intuition about them.

Do not step into this belief that your gut is going to tell you to run in opposite directions when you satisfy suspect people. It would be a small, easy push.

I simply know that I had this unexpected revulsion for the driver. In this case, I simply desired to get out of his cab. It merely made me feel like there was something incorrect about being in the cab.

In the same way, your impulses would speak to you using a language you know. Whether it is chilled down your spinal column, goosebumps, or just an unexpected need to throw up, you will recognize that feeling when you experience it, and with practice, you will learn to trust it.

Use the best practices in all your dealings
"Good, better, best.

Never allow it to rest until your good is better, and your much better is best." - St. Jerome.

The Christians have a saying, "you reap what you sow". It is more than merely a scriptural phrase. It encapsulates the natural order of things. We know the terrible things in some cases, happen to good people and vice versa. However, never believe for one minute that people do not get their comeuppance because they do. You naturally want to shut yourself in and close yourself off to people when you have been dealt with severely in life. And if you need to deal with people, you want to position yourself where you would have the upper hand continually. The problem with this kind of thinking is that because of your experiences; you end up being a victim who has made a choice [at least on a subconscious level] to make other people victims.

You may be able to find short-lived satisfaction in dealing with the same card that other people have dealt you to innocent people; however, the damage, in the long run, can be ravaging. Plus, you could wind up setting off a chain of occasions with a cause and effect that might come back to you. Even when you are presented with the chance, do not take it. Instead, turn the circumstance around by choosing to end the discomfort cycle with you. As someone who has been here, I can tell you that it is not easy. As a teenager, I was painfully shy. I found it difficult to speak to people. Even when I was with people like my moms, dads, brother, or sister who I have known all my life, I didn't crawl out of my shell.

All that changed when I satisfied Debbie. She was my high school love and I keep in mind being painfully in love with her.

It took a lot of psychological energy to summon up the courage to ask her out finally. And when I did, I was even more blown away by the reality that she said yes. I was walking on sunlight for the next three months until I discovered that I was simply a bet. Yes, I know it sounds remarkably like that teen film that was a hit back in the day other than this time, I was the victim. It hurt more than words can say, and that was not the worst part. I was humiliated by the worst way people like me can be. You understand that dream will have where you are to present a speech in front of the whole school, and you all see yourself naked suddenly? This was way worse than that.

I am unsure how I could get through that month in school much less the whole academic year, but I did. Quick forward to my post-college years, I met Debbie once again. Let us just say I remained in a more advantageous position, and I had the option of using my office to make her life tough, but I chose not to. Initially, she analyzed this to mean I still had feelings for her, and she tried to work that to her advantage. I pleasantly told her that I was simply doing my job. I would have reacted differently if I had held on to the feelings that I had for her in the past. It was either she would have been successful in her attempts to seduce me, or I would have been tempted into using the powers that my position prefers to "penalize" her. But I did neither. And in that decision, I discovered real flexibility.

Life has a funny way of working itself out. Instead, arm yourself with the lessons you have learned and use it to your advantage.

When you are put to the test, your best comes out.

CONCLUSION

Life is about making decisions. While many fear to have limitations, the significance of having life limits supersedes their absence. As an individual, a couple, or a family, you need to recognize some worths in life.

Borders must be definite. You do not need me with restrictions in life as a sense of punishment. Negative limits are produced without worth addition in mind.

Social circles in life should always tune to one's personal goals and not the other way round. This underscores the need to come up with clear boundaries that will assist you in growing toward your goals in life. Family, partners, workmates, and friends will always support your borders so long as they are favorable and transparent.

I have heard people issue out the caution saying: "the heart of guy is frantically wicked". I don't know who said it or where I heard it, but it is stuck in my head, and I discover it to be real. There are no gadgets or software applications that a person can use to decipher the thoughts of another person. The best you can do is understand your thoughts and feelings and do your best to live out your concepts and worths. Just because you can't tell if your new best friend is betraying you or not should not mean you need to spend your days pondering over it.

Men's capacity to do well is similarly as terrific as it is to go the other way, and this is not the best part. The best part is that for every single person who has hurt you in the past, there are a hundred more who want to do good to you.

On the contrary, I composed it to help you make better options in your relationships.

And if individuals have actually hurt you, this book is suggested to help you with the recovery process. Nothing in life is ever concluded. If you take the lessons that I have shared with you into practice, you can effectively open yourself to the fantastic prospects life has in store for you.

Close this book, but keep your heart and mind open. A few of the clichés in life have a remarkable impact on our lives. Love hard, smile more, and let go.

Life is too sweet and too precious to live it any other way. And always wake up with the pointer that you should have the best that life has to offer. Thank you for taking me on this journey with you.

CPSIA information can be obtained
at www.ICGtesting.com
Printed in the USA
BVHW041016021120
592327BV00008B/218